Squinting

to See the **Rainbow**

Trusting the Promises of God
in Our Darkest Days

DWIGHT AND TABITHA EASLER

Squinting to See the Rainbow:
Trusting the Promises of God in Our Darkest Days

All Scripture references are from the New King James Version (NKJV), unless otherwise noted.

ISBN: 978-1-940645-99-5

Greenville, South Carolina

PUBLISHED IN THE UNITED STATES OF AMERICA

THIS BOOK IS DEDICATED TO THE FOLLOWING:

— Seth, Matthew, and Hannah, who have shown us the grace of perseverance and faith through adversity. They have been the proof that God works for good.

— Our parents, who grieved quietly to shield our hearts.

— Our Corinth Church family, community friends, and caring strangers who offered shoulders to cry on, resources, love, and stories of pain and comfort — their very lives — to help us through the darkness of grief.

— Those on the Cleveland Park miniature train who suffered greatly with us and persevered by faith, and the good Samaritans, first responders and hospitalist who gave their all and saved lives on March 19, 2011.

— The little ones in Benji's kindergarten class who wrote memories of Benji for us before they graduated from kindergarten in 2011. They stole our hearts again in 2019 when they left eighth grade by refusing to forget Benji, leaving his chair open and requesting that the principal read off his name as a fellow graduate. Their love and faithfulness to their kindergarten friend cannot be measured.

— In memory of our precious Benji, who brought so much joy and delight to our family and who still brings smiles to our faces.

— In thankfulness to God for lending us Benji for six beautiful years and for extending His grace and faithfulness to us in countless, undeserved ways.

FOREWORD

When Dwight Easler told me he and his wife were going to write a book about trusting God through the most difficult of times, I thought to myself, "I don't know of anyone I've ever met who is more equipped by God's grace to write that book than my friends Dwight and Tabitha."

I met Dwight when he was a college student. He was good friends with a staff member at the church where I served as senior pastor. Even then, I was impressed with the great spiritual maturity I recognized in him. When he eventually married the love of his life, Tabitha, and soon started raising a family, I was blessed to see how this young family always made it a point to do things God's way.

I was preaching revival services at Corinth Baptist Church, where Dwight serves as senior pastor, when his son Benji was born. None of us could possibly have known how soon the joy of Benji's birth, and the absolute delight of his personality, would be cut short by tragedy. In *Squinting to See the Rainbow,* Dwight and Tabitha Easler share from their hearts, their experience and, ultimately, from God's Word about how God is still good, even when circumstances are bad.

One word that I have heard from others and have used myself more than any other to describe the Easler family and the horror of Benji's death is … grace. God's grace. Grace to go on. Grace to trust. Grace to still believe. Grace to live. Tragedy sometimes tears a family apart, but because of grace, the Easlers have drawn closer — closer to each other, and closer to the Almighty God of endless grace.

I don't know who first used the phrase, "God can turn misery into ministry," but I know I have seen that truth lived out in the entire Easler family. If you will read the words of this book with an open heart and open mind, you will be ministered to, blessed by, and equipped for a lifetime of "Trusting the Promises of God in [Your] Darkest Days." Habakkuk 3:17-18 says, "Though the fig tree may not blossom, nor fruit be on the vines; though the labor of the olive may fail, and the fields yield no food; though the flock may be cut off from the fold, and there be no herd in the stalls — yet I will rejoice in the Lord, I will joy in the God of my salvation."

Believe. Trust.

Squint — by faith — and you'll see the rainbow.

Gary E. Rogers, Pastor
Chaplain, South Carolina Firefighters Association

INTRODUCTION

Tabitha and I sat in our living room with a news reporter who was interviewing us about the Cleveland Park train accident that claimed our youngest son's life. Our two other sons were in the hallway, just around the corner, as we tried to answer the reporter's questions. Matthew had stitches around his eyes, and he and Seth had casts on both arms. They were playing with birthday presents. Matthew's birthday was just six days after the worst moment of our lives: 1:04 p.m., March 19, 2011.

For all of us, the house was too quiet, and the boys weren't playing as rambunctiously as they normally would. Everyone knew why, but we couldn't speak it. The truth was too crushing. Yes, they hurt from their injuries, but the familiar voice of their little brother Benji yelling and pouncing on them in battle was not there anymore.

The reporter asked questions, and we did our best to describe Benji and give him a voice in the injustice of the moment. It was also a chance to share hope with others, but it tore us to pieces inside to talk about it. I remember the reporter saying sweetly as she left, "Your story will help someone. Thank you for sharing with us."

As time went by, many people from the church, community, and state — and even around the nation — wrote cards, sent books and sat with us as we cried. The people who shared their stories were opening their hearts in order to help us. And now the Lord has impressed upon our hearts to do the same for you. We want you to know and remember our bubbly little boy, Benji — who, it seems, left us too early — but we also want you to know that you can have hope and live by faith even when nothing makes sense around you.

This book has been an on-and-off journey for us. Grief, trauma, and life had to be worked out before we could say many of the things we wanted to say in this book. In the end, I am thankful for the time. There are things I know now that I didn't know then, and Tabitha's, Matthew's and even Hannah's contributions to this book are evidence of God's work in ways that I could not possibly have communicated by myself. When I see my oldest son, Seth, in his firefighter uniform leaving to go to work at one of the busiest fire stations in Greenville, South Carolina, my heart is filled with thankfulness, knowing that life could have gone so much differently and negatively for our family. The Lord allowed us to be broken as a family on March 19, 2011, and He began to reshape us that day in ways we still do not fully grasp.

A book that was given to me shortly after Benji's death was *When Heaven Is Silent*, by Ron Dunn. You will see it quoted a few times in this book. I credit this book with keeping me in faith and letting me know that it was all right to feel the things that I felt in grief. As I journeyed with Dunn in his book, I found myself weeping with him and believing with Jacob, Job, and Paul in their suffering. I found myself trusting God's sovereignty even when I despaired for my life in grief.

Our desire for you is to find hope within the pages of this book that can help you in your darkest days and the years that follow. We want you to know that you can see the rainbow of God's Word and God's presence even against the backdrop of your darkest days. May the Lord grant you faith, hope, and comfort in the journey ahead.

Dwight Easler
October 2019

Squinting

to See the **Rainbow**

Trusting the Promises of God
in Our Darkest Days

SECTION 1
DWIGHT

GOD'S GRACE

Squinting to See the Rainbow

And so it was, as her soul was departing (for she died), that she called his name Ben-Oni; but his father called him Benjamin. (Genesis 35:18)

I cannot read this verse without thinking of a bright little boy with a boisterous laugh. He was a tough little fellow who always liked to get rough with me and his brothers. He would act really mad when his brothers would laugh and joke and say that their momma, who was expecting our fourth child, was fat. He was always on my team in football and would brave the tackles of his big brothers. I remember the feel of his sweaty little palm as he held my hand to walk home from church or from a playground somewhere.

I remember him helping me to put the crib together for his soon-expected sister, Hannah. He was ready to see the little sister whom he named after his friend in kindergarten. He said, "It's such a sweet name, and Hannahs always turn out beautiful."

I remember how I carried him to bed for the last time after I had been gone all afternoon with a high school fire academy class. He was asleep on the floor with a stomachache after eating too many doughnuts.

All of those great memories flood back as I remember Benji. I can hardly type these words without stopping for tears. It has been a painful journey to write this. It has been a struggle — with traumatic images, memories, spiritual questions and, generally, thoughts of my own inadequacy to even speak to these things. I have fought through years of wondering about what I remember and why I can't remember pieces of the accident that changed our lives and took Benji from us — at least on this earth. The Lord has given me a sense of peace to share these things with the hope that it will encourage you and build your faith.

The context of the Genesis passage above is Jacob meeting and being changed by the Lord. Jacob had met the Lord at Bethel, and his name was changed from Jacob (or, "one who grabs the heel") to Israel (or, "prince with God"). He did not know that the next steps in his life would bring terrible tragedy and turmoil. The woman he loved would die in childbirth, and the child would be named the "son of my sorrow." Jacob, seeing Rachel in the eyes of the little boy, named him Benjamin, "son of my right hand."

It is often that way in life. The Lord prepares us for things we cannot see, by way of victories we didn't know we needed. Jacob would need to know the Lord's promises in the years to come in order to survive physically, mentally, emotionally and spiritually.

Looking back over the years, I can see the same sovereign work in my life. I have tried many times in the last few years to write, only to be overcome with grief and discouragement. I write this book for God's glory, for the memory of Benji, for my family and my church family — and for you, in your grief. I write this because the late Bill Poore, my pastor and friend, gave me what I needed to keep going when I was almost destroyed in grief and struggle. I pray that you will hear my heart and remember Benji when you read these words and that you will be encouraged in the knowledge that God can fulfill His promises.

In 2010, my three growing sons were busy playing with the toys they had gotten for Christmas. We had a very rare snow on the ground that Christmas, and the boys had the blessing of extra time to play. That summer, we had been able to take the boys to Disney World before the meeting of the Southern Baptist Convention. Benji, our youngest son, had started kindergarten and was getting big enough to really come into his own, roughhousing with Seth and Matthew. Other regular activities at our house included throwing balls at each other, wrestling, playing football and shooting darts at one other. In January after that Christmas of 2010, I had the blessing of baptizing Benji, who had trusted Jesus earlier during one of our times together as a family. We were expecting another child, and to our surprise we found out it would be a girl. The boys were so excited to be able to welcome a baby sister into the family. I look back on 2010 as a high point in my life, like the moment Jacob had on Bethel. The world seemed so right. I didn't know what 2011 would bring.

On March 19, 2011, after a fun day at a pottery painting shop, our family, along with fifteen children and parents from our church, went to Cleveland Park in Spartanburg, South Carolina, to ride the miniature train. Just that day, the train had started its operation. (On my bookshelf is a picture of Benji and Trey Burgess sitting on the train. Two seats behind them, you can see me smiling.) Four minutes after boarding the train, I was lying on the ragged rocks of a creek bank, trying to regain my senses and find my family.

The train conductor had gone into the second curve of the track three times faster than he should have, sending twenty-nine passengers plunging into a rocky creek. It was so sudden that I barely had time to think of how dangerous it felt. The pain of a busted head and a dislocated ankle was soon numbed by the crushing ache of grief and helplessness.

Benji suffered head and internal trauma, which caused him to go into cardiac arrest. I held his foot and prayed as some Good Samaritans worked to help him. Tabitha, my wife, who was almost eight months pregnant, was ejected from the train and knocked briefly unconscious. As she gathered herself, she had to see the unthinkable. Matthew and Seth were later rushed away to the hospital with arm and facial injuries, not knowing where we were or what had happened to anyone else.

The horror of the next hours and days is deeply painful to recall — even now, more than eight years later. There are things worse than death for the believer in Christ. Seeing my son dying, telling his brothers that he had died, seeing my little boy in a casket, and hearing my wife cry and wish she could feel Benji's face again — recalling it all is still more than I can take. It causes me to shed tears when I am alone.

I can write these things now because I can say to you that the Lord is faithful. The promises that I trusted in those early days are real and powerful. The Lord can — and will — work for good. However, you may not be able to see that now. As it was for me, the blur of tragedy may be blocking your vision.

As I was thinking about all this one day, something I used to do as a child came to mind. I would go out into the yard and spray the water hose into the hot, sunny July sky. Sometimes, if the spray was just right, I could squint and, through my eyelashes, see a rainbow. In the years since the train accident, almost every day I have walked by Benji's last kindergarten drawing, dated March 2011, which we found in his book bag a few days after the accident. It's a drawing of a rainbow, and Benji is riding a unicorn on the rainbow. Underneath the rainbow is his precious signature.

There have been so many times I tried to remember how good those years were before 2011, and especially how good 2010 was — the year before it all changed. That wonderful trip to Disney and the laughs we shared that week. The day Benji stomped on the guy's foot in the Mickey Mouse costume to make sure he was real. All the memories start well, only to be blocked by the images of my son's broken body on a creek bank.

In my mind, the heat of the tragedy is too much. The only thing I can do is spray my soul with the water of God's Word and squint into the Word to see the rainbow.

I want you to know that you can — and you will — see that rainbow. He is the God of all comfort, and He is the God who intervenes in our darkest days. He has sustained me through these years, even though I am left broken and, many times, still darkened by tragedy.

You are not alone in your journey. Look into the water of God's Word and see the rainbow of His promises. You will see the same things Jacob saw — and that I have seen. Second Corinthians 4:7-8 says, "But we have this treasure in earthen vessels, that the excellence of the power may be of God and not of us. We are hard pressed on every side, yet not crushed; we are perplexed, but not in despair."

WHERE IS THE GOD OF ELIJAH?

And Elisha saw it, and he cried out, "My father, my father, the chariot of Israel and its horsemen!" So he saw him no more. And he took hold of his own clothes and tore them into two pieces. He also took up the mantle of Elijah that had fallen from him, and went back and stood by the bank of the Jordan. (2 Kings 2:12-13)

I chose the passage above for Benji's funeral. As Elisha stood by the brook, he saw his father in the faith, Elijah, taken up. As I read this passage in the foggy time between the day of the accident and the day of the Benji's funeral, I moved away from the horrific images of seeing Benji dying on the creek bank, and I looked, in faith, to Benji being taken up in glory to see his heavenly home.

Like Elisha, I found myself in grief, clinging to my son's clothing, his picture, his memory, the sound of his voice, the feel of his hair or his fingers wrapped around my chin as he rode on my shoulders. Like Elisha, I was stuck in the middle, between a fallen world and the hope of glory. "Where is the God of Elijah?" Where is God when you are standing on the creek bank and your world has crashed in? He is there, and He will show His power. However, that does not mean the pain of your loss will be erased. Elisha still had to go on without Elijah.

Maybe the mantle of the prophet still held the smell of the old man and reminded Elisha of the voice of the prophet. I remember the clothes and stuffed animals that Tabitha and I clung to after the accident. I remember the voicemail on Tab's phone of Benji saying, "I called you, Momma," which we listened to with joy and with tears. The fear of losing that smell, that voice, that memory still lingers in our souls to this day.

Maybe all of these grief points were in Elisha's life as well, but the Lord planned to do mighty things in Elisha's life. The God of Elijah was there and would prove Himself strong and powerful in Elisha's life. Looking back, I can see the Lord was there when I was lying beside that creek calling out to Him to save my child and to help my other two sons who being dashed away in ambulances.

I prayed with torn clothes, holding onto the little foot of Benji and looking at his face for any signs of life. Images and feelings rush back as I type these words, images that I cannot unsee: Blood and bruising on Benji's lifeless body. Matthew standing helplessly in the distance, his eyes swelling shut. The screams of people around me. The soft voice of Tabitha standing beside the EMS workers, holding her belly and telling Benji, "It's okay, baby. Mommy is here with you."

Even now my heart cries out, "Where is the God of Elijah?" Where is the God my son trusted and professed his faith to so joyfully in baptism just two months earlier? Now, like then, I know that He is here. He is working to bring His children to glory and empower those who are left behind. The Lord is glorified in both. By faith in the resurrection of Jesus, I know that Benji traded a train for a chariot that day. As my pastor said in the funeral message, "We do not know what the Lord saved Benji from that day by letting him go to heaven at six years old. Neither do we know what the Lord is saving us from through this moment." Looking back over the years since Benji died, I can say those words redefined my life as I looked intently to see God's empowerment and work in my family and ministry.

The day before the funeral, I held my son Matthew in the lobby of the funeral home and asked him if he wanted to go in and see his brother in the casket. He refused to go in. Eventually his crying stopped, and he said with the voice of childlike faith, "He isn't there. He is in heaven." My heart rejoiced as I held him and cried with him. His birthday was coming up soon. His arms were in a cast, and his eyes had stitches above them. He looked so helpless, but I saw the heart of a faith warrior coming forth. Just a few days before, when they were rolled into the hospital room after surgery, Matthew and Seth cried and asked where Benji was. Matthew sobbed beside me in the bed and cried out in the night, "This is just a dream!" Now, in this moment, he was teaching me what God can do through childlike faith, how He can work through unspeakable loss to bring about a new prophet in Israel.

Just this week I was looking back over camera recordings to help a church member find a lost item in one of the educational rooms. On one of the videos was my sixteen-year-old son and his friend on their knees an hour before the service, praying for revival. I was reminded again of the answer to the question posed so long ago: "Where is the God of Elijah?" He is here, and He is working. When all else fails, He will not.

The Blessing of Brokenness

Then Jacob was left alone; and a Man wrestled with him until the breaking of day. Now when He saw that He did not prevail against him, He touched the socket of his hip; and the socket of Jacob's hip was out of joint as He wrestled with him. And He said, "Let Me go, for the day breaks." But he said, "I will not let You go unless You bless me!" So He said to him, "What is your name?" He said, "Jacob." And He said, "Your name shall no longer be called Jacob, but Israel; for you have struggled with God and with men, and have prevailed." Then Jacob asked, saying, "Tell me Your name, I pray." And He said, "Why is it that you ask about My name?" And He blessed him there. And Jacob called the name of the place Peniel: "For I have seen God face to face, and my life is preserved." Just as he crossed over Peniel the sun rose on him, and he limped on his hip. (Genesis 32:24-31)

Bill and Patsy Poore took us into their church and ministry when we moved to seminary in 1995 and became special friends. After those years, Dr. Poore was a special speaker in the churches I pastored, and we spoke almost once a week. He was a constant source of humor and advice. When his son Jay passed away suddenly in his thirties, I saw my friend and pastor shrink in grief. He struggled with questions he could not answer. His transparency during that time was vitally important in ways that I could not imagine. The Lord was using the grief of my pastor to teach me lessons I did not want to learn.

After Benji died, he agreed to come and fill the pulpit in our church for a few weeks until we could get things back together. He and Patsy came to see us, and he brought me a book by Ron Dunn called *When Heaven Is Silent*. He told me that the thoughts in that book helped him through the grief and unanswered questions in the days after Jay had passed. The book became dear to me. I read about the journey of grief and faith that Dunn had taken after his son Ronnie Jr.'s death. The transparent thoughts and the sometimes dark truths of the Bible jumped out at me from those pages. How a believer can go through such a dark night of the soul and still totally trust the Lord was real and encouraging to me. Reading the Old Testament books of Genesis and Job as Dunn plunged into the truths of living in brokenness and faith all at the same time was like a lifeline to my soul. The account of Jacob wrestling with God became dear to me, I believe, because of the limp. In the days after the train accident I struggled with a dislocated ankle. The doctors reset it and waited for the swelling to go down to see if there was anything they could do to help with the torn ligaments and tendons. The helpless feeling of being broken in body and spirit was a reality for me.

As I read through Genesis, I was brought again to the statement in the funeral service: "We do not know what the Lord saved Benji from by allowing him to go to heaven at six years old, and we do not know what the Lord is saving us from." Many times in his life, Jacob had tried to control his life by his own decisions. The Lord had worked in His sovereignty many times to bless Jacob in spite of himself. In Genesis 32, Jacob was about to meet Esau, his brother. Jacob developed a plan to try to appeal to the heartstrings of Esau, knowing that Esau had wanted him dead for many years.

That night near Peniel, Jacob met someone he could not overpower with wit. A long battle ensued, and by the end of the night Jacob was left clinging to the one he was fighting. Jacob didn't need more of Jacob, he needed more of the Lord. That is what brokenness leaves us with. When we reach the place of brokenness, we cling to the Lord. The Lord taught me through this passage the blessings of brokenness. The Lord had to break Jacob to remake him into Israel, to show him — and us — that promises are often fulfilled in painful ways. If everything we did in our finite wisdom always worked out, then we would not be prepared for the things that are coming. The Lord blesses us by breaking us, saving us from the Esaus to come. The limp is used for our good so that we may cross the brook with the sun at our back, knowing that we have met God, and He is with us.

As Jacob limped toward Esau, the Bible shows us the wisdom of the Almighty. The man approaching his brother with hundreds of armed men did not see a self-confident schemer any longer. He saw a haggard, broken person limping across that plain, bowing before his brother. The result was that "then he crossed over before them and bowed himself to the ground seven times, until he came near to his brother. But Esau ran to meet him, and embraced him, and fell on his neck and kissed him, and they wept" (Genesis 33:3-4).

What a powerful lesson in brokenness. God breaks us to make us new and to prepare us for the Esaus to come. God can use the limp to create something greater in our lives. I can say with certainty that the Lord has taught me many lessons through my broken heart. Some days are like that long night, wrestling with the Lord. I do not want what my brokenness brings. I do not want the limp, but I cling to the One who gave it to me, knowing that I cannot handle what I thought I could handle. I limp with the sun at my back, knowing that the Lord is changing me for good.

Will the limp of grief and loss ever go away? Most people I have asked say no. A retired pastor who had walked through days of grief after his wife of many years had died of cancer said to me, "The tears you shed will drop from your eyes to heal someone you do not know." That truth was definitely proven to me in the lives of others. The tears they shed and the faith they expressed helped bring healing to me and my family.

My prayer is that our tears will help bring healing to others. Be encouraged to know that, however your brokenness may come, the Lord can use it to prepare you for what is ahead.

But God

And Joseph said to his brothers, "Please come near to me." So they came near. Then he said: "I am Joseph your brother, whom you sold into Egypt. But now, do not therefore be grieved or angry with yourselves because you sold me here; for God sent me before you to preserve life." ... Joseph said to them, "Do not be afraid, for am I in the place of God? But as for you, you meant evil against me; but God meant it for good, in order to bring it about as it is this day, to save many people alive." (Genesis 45:4-5; 50:19-20)

In January and February of 2011 the Lord led me to preach through the life of Joseph in an eight-week series of messages. The last message was based upon the verses at the beginning of this chapter. The title of that message was "A Moment of Greatness." Joseph had a moment of greatness when he was able to look beyond his past, forgive his brothers and see God's purpose in the adversity he endured.

This sermon was very easy to preach as a celebration of God's sovereign purpose. However, just a few weeks later, in the hospital, I thought of this message and how I didn't want that kind of moment. I wanted my son back. I wanted my life back. I wanted life to go back to the way it was.

Maybe Joseph felt that way for many years. As he was suffering as a slave, or being falsely accused, or put in prison as an innocent man, surely he must have thought about how he wanted his life back as the favorite son of Jacob. Why did it have to be this way?

It also struck me, looking back, how I did not have an appropriate timeline in my head to see that it took years of prayers and life experience to get to Genesis 45. Would I ever be able to see the purpose of the tragedy that struck our lives? Would I be able to see any part of God's purpose?

In all of these questions, I kept coming back to the great transition of this verse: "But God." This became a pivotal faith activity for me in order to keep myself from plunging into the darkness of grief. What had happened was terrible. The pain that Tabitha, the boys and I were facing with our church and family could not be made good.

But God.

God had a plan, in His power, to work for good in the midst of evil. I considered how this played out in the life of Joseph. I thought of the things that had to take place in his life for him to make sense of his tragic circumstances. First, he acknowledged evil — the evil intentions of his brothers, the evil he had suffered, and the evil circumstances that brought them to Egypt and put them back together again. I began to see that we must accept the fallen nature of our world to see how God can work in it — not to accept it in a fatalistic way, as Solomon presents the world under the sun in the book of Ecclesiastes, but to accept that things happen in this fallen world that the Lord allows and uses for His glory and for our good.

Jesus pointed to the nature of our world in Luke 13, which begins with a question about a certain tragedy people had suffered: "There were present at that season some who told Him about the Galileans whose blood Pilate had mingled with their sacrifices. And Jesus answered and said to them, 'Do you suppose that these Galileans were worse sinners than all other Galileans, because they suffered such things? I tell you, no; but unless you repent you will all likewise perish. Or those eighteen on whom the tower in Siloam fell and killed them, do you think that they were worse sinners than all other men who dwelt in Jerusalem? I tell you, no; but unless you repent you will all likewise perish.'"

In this passage, we note some very obvious things about the response of Jesus. Jesus was not shocked by the tragic loss of life. Neither did He try to explain all the questions of "Why?" that must have been floating around. He did not try to defend God's actions in allowing it to happen. Jesus simply acknowledged the event, referenced another event, and then proclaimed to everyone that it could happen to them and they should be ready for eternity. By realizing this, a person can avoid the victim mentality. A person can understand, in this fallen world, that we all suffer in some ways, and our lives will end if the Lord does not return before we die.

If that is true, we can do two things. First, we can trust Christ as our Savior and Lord and turn from our sin. Second, we can live our lives knowing that, as a believer, God will not allow our suffering to be fruitless.

The story of Joseph is that of a person who readily acknowledged the evil he had suffered. He certainly did not talk about how good it felt to be sold as a slave, or how wonderful it was to be accused of rape, or how exhilarating it was to be in prison as an innocent man. No, he understood what that took from him. However, in the end, he was able to accept it all by acknowledging one great truth: "But God."

The second key to Joseph's moment is a God-centered perspective. He recognized the evil, but he kept his eyes on the Lord. He saw the Lord's hand at work. This has helped me so many times in these years of sorrow to avoid utter defeat. When I have felt the hopelessness creeping in, I have prayed simply, "Lord show me Your hand again. Show me how You are working." He has never failed.

I remember the first evidence of a "But God" moment: the birth of our daughter, Hannah, about a month after the train accident. On April 27, 2011, my wife, still bearing the scars of her injuries, gave birth to Hannah Hope, a perfectly healthy little baby girl who looked like her brothers and captured our hearts. In the days to come, we came to see that God had divinely orchestrated the timing of her birth to help us through our darkest days. Her sweet smile and her cuddly personality were a ministry to a momma who was hurting deeply. Tabitha said once, "I don't know if this baby will ever talk, because all she does is watch me cry."

Nowadays, watching Hannah at age eight is a huge "But God" truth. When she dances or wears a hat, she reminds me of Benji. Her smile and her personality reflect the love and the faith of her mother. She brags on her big brothers as though they were kings. We have said often that Hannah cannot replace Benji. However, the Lord sent a minister to our souls, born one month into our darkest night.

I also think of the people who have made professions of faith since 2011, or the young man who serves now as a faithful deacon. Days after the train accident, he called me, weeping, saying he wanted to repent and return to the Lord.

The years since March 19, 2011, have brought their share of struggle and pain. However, I can say that when I have looked to the Lord for His perspective, I have found His hand at work. This perspective has saved me from hopelessness and purposeless living.

Many useless things have been spoken to me that did not help me in my grief: "God needed another angel." "God has a reason." "God knew you could take it, so He took your child." Or, even, "I don't think God was paying attention, because He would not have let that happen." These terrible phrases, like many others, offer no comfort. However, Romans

8:28 offers real hope for the sufferer: "And we know that all things work together for good to those who love God, to those who are the called according to His purpose."

In these verses we find the key to a God-centered perspective. There is no exception clause in this verse. "We know" … is what Joseph knew from experience. And he could say, "But God," because God always works for good to those who love Him. For the unbeliever, the suffering in a fallen world is part of the curse. For the believer, the suffering becomes a channel of God's glory to make His power known.

There is one final truth in these verses that became the backbone of my faith in the difficult days. Joseph would not allow his circumstances to turn him inward. He saw that God allowed those things in order to save many people. His pain had a purpose for God's glory, and for others. His life didn't slip into fatalistic self-absorption. A victorious perspective was accomplished when he refused to make it about himself.

It is so easy when bad things happen to focus on ourselves, to pretend that we are the only ones who are hurting, or to act as though God has something against us. To do this is to rob ourselves of the opportunity for God to bear fruit through our suffering, which can help others.

It has taken me this long to write these words for a lot of reasons. Hurt, raising kids, pastoring a busy church, caring for sick parents, and general life-circumstances all come into play. However, what brings me back to it time and time again is the hurt I see and feel in the faces of others. Like the young woman who has suffered betrayal and divorce and the sudden death of her fiancé. Like the friend hurting after the death of his wife of fifty-two years, or the couple who lost two children in two years after childbirth. What has brought me back to this through the years is an earnest desire to keep seeing the Lord's hand at work and a desire to help the hurting.

The desire to see the hurting has opened my eyes to the good the Lord can bring through the fallen world and to boldly proclaim, "But God!" My prayer is that you can experience that today. Acknowledge the evil you have suffered, look at it through a God-centered perspective, and see how, through it, the Lord can be glorified and people can be helped.

CARRY MY BONES:
DISAPPOINTMENT AND HOPE

Then Joseph took an oath from the children of Israel, saying, "God will surely visit you, and you shall carry up my bones from here." So Joseph died, being one hundred and ten years old; and they embalmed him, and he was put in a coffin in Egypt. (Genesis 50:25-26)

The results of the perspective laid out in the Scripture above are obvious in the next verses. As Joseph was dying, his words were very telling. Even at 110, he still felt the sting of not being able to go home again. He understood how God had worked for good in his circumstances, but that did not change his disappointment.

This was something that I also had to come to grips with. It is possible to see God's hand at work and to trust Him but still live with the nagging disappointment about the way you wished it could have been. No doubt, Job felt this way. You cannot read the book of Job without hearing the disappointment in his voice over his circumstances. The horror of his circumstances were the reality of his greatest fear. He said, "For my sighing comes before I eat, and my groanings pour out like water. For the thing I greatly feared has come upon me, and what I dreaded has happened to me" (Job 3:24-25).

I have often wondered if, when the dust settled in Job's life, he ever sat and thought about how things might have been. We have the full story now, thousands of years later, and Job had the eternal reality of the results of God's victory over Satan in his suffering. But it still did not erase the pain — or the ten graves he stood beside while he was on the earth.

Joseph's prophetic understanding that God would fulfill His promise to Israel was mixed with the disappointment that he would not see it. Going forward in healing after tragedy and loss involves living with the sting of a sudden life-change that never will be reversed. Reading the words of Joseph in Genesis 50:25 ("God will surely visit you, and you shall carry up my bones from here"), we realize that this loss goes on as long as we walk the earth. That sting of "what could have been" lives within my wife and me every time we see Benji's kindergarten classmates step up to another grade. We smile, we hug, and we tell them we are proud, but in the back of our minds are always questions: What would Benji look like? How good of a student would he be? Would he have a girlfriend?

To our daughter, Benji will always be the little boy she can never touch. He will never be the big brother who could tell her he chose her name because "Hannahs are always beautiful."

The remarkable thing about Joseph was that he could look beyond personal disappointment to something far greater. As Paul says, "For I consider that the sufferings of this present time are not worthy to be compared with the glory which shall be revealed in us" (Romans 8:18). Joseph took the long view. Yes, all of the things that had happened to him were terrible and painful, yet God had worked powerfully to use him as part of the fulfillment of His promises to Israel, and there was more to come. After Joseph left this life behind, God would still be working for His glory.

I have thought about this many times through these years. When I struggle with the long view is when I am at my worst. When it seems the pain is strongest and deepest is when I forget what God has done and what He is going to do. In those times, I have to return to the message of Joseph. I have to look at my life — my "bone box" — and realize that the Lord is working sovereignly, even beyond my lifetime, to do things I cannot understand, or even know.

The words of Job in his darkest moments show us how to take the long view. He says, "Oh, that my words were written! Oh, that they were inscribed in a book! That they were engraved on a rock with an iron pen and lead, forever! For I know that my Redeemer lives, and He shall stand at last on the earth; and after my skin is destroyed, this I know, that in my flesh I shall see God, Whom I shall see for myself, and my eyes shall behold, and not another. How my heart yearns within me!" (Job 19:23-27). In these times of agony and disappointment, Job longs for someone to record his plight. However, he almost instantly transitions to an eternal perspective, and he takes the long view of what God is going to do. A powerful result occurs at this moment in the text. He stops complaining and starts praising.

Recently I was standing beside our worship leader, waiting to pray when the congregation finished singing "In Christ Alone." As we sang, out of the corner of my eye I saw my wife with a smile on her face, her eyes closed and her head raised to heaven, singing. My eyes filled with tears, remembering how she had chosen that song to end the funeral service for Benji. Now, eight years later, I did not see a mother defeated in grief. I saw a mom who had just celebrated Christmas once again without her boy, but who had the long view that one day she would hold him again. "No guilt in life, no fear of death, this is the power of Christ in me."

We all carry with us disappointment and pain, but, with an eternal perspective, we know that the sufferings of this life cannot be compared to the glory to come. God gives us that glorious victory when we trust Him in the trials of life. The result of Joseph's faith and eternal perspective lasted 400 years. Exodus 13:19 says, "And Moses took the bones of Joseph with him, for he had placed the children of Israel under solemn oath, saying, 'God will surely visit you, and you shall carry up my bones from here with you.'"

Our prayer should be that we might be transparent in our disappointments, but not bitter. How do we avoid bitterness? By having an eternal perspective. We can hold onto the truth that God is doing something bigger than us, something we will only see in eternity through Christ.

We can trust Him to work for good in spite of the evil intentions of others and the circumstances of a fallen world, where suffering and death exist. One of the first times I experienced this powerful perspective was at a yard sale hosted by our church to help the victims of the train accident with their medical expenses. A young man came that day with his aunt. He looked like he had been up all night and smelled like cigarettes. After a while, his aunt asked me if I would talk to him in private. He began to talk about Benji dying and how that made him think about how he was living. At first I fought against the idea of talking about Benji, because I didn't want to talk about my little boy dying the way he did. But as we continued to talk, I realized this hardened young man was being softened to the gospel by the death of Benji. That day, the young man prayed for God to forgive him and save him.

In September 2012 I conducted that young man's funeral. His death was sad and tragic, but the Lord let me see His power through Benji's death. The faith and testimony of a six-year-old, including his dying and going to heaven, broke through to a young man who had given himself to drugs and alcohol — and brought him to Christ.

Can you believe that God can use your disappointment and suffering for His glory? Can you believe that God can bring people to salvation through what you have gone through? If you can, your legacy may still be reaching someone for Christ long after you are gone.

THE POWER OF FORGIVENESS

Joseph said to them, "Do not be afraid, for am I in the place of God? But as for you, you meant evil against me; but God meant it for good, in order to bring it about as it is this day, to save many people alive." (Genesis 50:19-20)

"Give us this day our daily bread. And forgive us our debts, As we forgive our debtors." (Matthew 6:11-12)

"And when he had begun to settle accounts, one was brought to him who owed him ten thousand talents. But as he was not able to pay, his master commanded that he be sold, with his wife and children and all that he had, and that payment be made. The servant therefore fell down before him, saying, 'Master, have patience with me, and I will pay you all.' Then the master of that servant was moved with compassion, released him, and forgave him the debt. But that servant went out and found one of his fellow servants who owed him a hundred denarii; and he laid hands on him and took him by the throat, saying, 'Pay me what you owe!' And his master was angry, and delivered him to the torturers until he should pay all that was due to him. So My heavenly Father also will do to you if each of you, from his heart, does not forgive his brother his trespasses." (Matthew 18:24-28; 34-35)

Almost immediately after the train accident, we were faced with a huge test of our faith and fortitude. We were trying to recover from our injuries, and we were grieving. We were also worried about our surviving boys, our unborn baby, our aging parents, and a church family and community in absolute shock. In the midst of this was a giant public disaster. This historic park and train ride had injured twenty-nine people and had killed my son. Reporters from local television stations and newspapers were calling everyone they could find. They were asking what was going to be done to the train operator, the parks department, the state, the city — really, anyone involved. It was a blur of activity as we tried to respond in grace to every person seeking answers. It was a constant struggle for balance in seeking justice for Benji, preventing such a thing from happening again, and trying to act biblically for the sake of my family and church.

A couple days after the accident, a surprising thing happened. I received a message that the train operator wanted to talk to me. After a few minutes, I called him, and his sister answered the phone. She told me that he was distraught and wanted to talk to me. A man with a shaky voice got on the phone and, between sobs, told me how sorry he was that Benji had died. Something happened as I listened, nothing short of miraculous. The Lord in that moment took anger out of me and gave me the ability to talk to the man about forgiveness. I don't remember everything I said, but I do remember saying something like, "I know Benji loved Jesus. Jesus died on the cross for my sin and your sin, and if He loves us enough to do that, then I know that I can love and forgive you." I still, to this day, credit the Lord for those words, because I would not have said them without God's power and Word. I am thankful for that moment.

The period of the next almost-three years was not as easy. Information about negligent supervision, people hiding behind their positions, politicians promising but not acting, all caused my anger to grow to a bitter level. We filed a wrongful death lawsuit along with the other victims to challenge the state of South Carolina to pay for the medical expenses and pain and suffering of the families involved. The case took over two years to resolve. At the end of the settlement negotiations, I left still angry that some of the people directly involved in oversight of the park were still employed and never really said they were sorry.

About a year later, a community leader called me to his office and told me he was organizing a rebuild of the park. County employees showed me the drawings and asked for our input. All of my struggles with unforgiveness and bitterness came back. I struggled to keep a positive attitude but felt I needed to be a part of the process in order to remember Benji and give him a voice.

The leader of the project was a Christian businessman in Spartanburg, and he asked me to share with the volunteers and county employees our story during the lunch breaks each day. I reluctantly said yes, and I talked about Benji and how the Lord had worked to help us through the years after the accident. I spoke one day about the blessing of brokenness. Afterwards, a young man stood over in the corner, sheepishly looking my direction. One of the leaders of the project came to me and said that the young man wanted to speak to me. I agreed, and as soon as he told me his name my mind flooded with things I told myself I would say to him if I ever saw him. Standing in front of me was the park supervisor. During depositions and presentations of evidence, his name came up several times, and some of the things that were brought out made me angry, knowing that what happened to Benji was entirely preventable. I was ready to unload.

When he started speaking, I realized the person in my imagination was being replaced by a young man who was heartbroken. He started by saying that he was prohibited from speaking to me for a long time and could not communicate how sorry he was for what had happened. He told me how, each day, he worked to keep something from happening to another child in the county parks. He said they had two objectives in the rebuild of the park: to make it the safest in South Carolina, and to remember Benji. As he said those words, tears were welling in his eyes, and he told me about his small children.

Once again, the Lord brought me to a dilemma of faith. I realized that God had brought me there that day to put me in front of the person I had not forgiven. I had chosen to blame his mistakes most for the accident. I had to choose in that moment whether to keep carrying my chain of bitterness and hate, or to drop it and be free. (I know many Christian people who still carry their chain.) In order to drop that chain, one must be helped to do so. For me, that help came through a simple leading from God to pray with that young man. I put my hand on his shoulder, and I prayed for his children to grow in the grace and knowledge of Jesus and to grow to be mighty warriors for Christ. I prayed for his children even though I knew that what he failed to notice contributed to my son's death. I shook his hand, and I have never encountered him again.

I have returned to the park only two times since, even though they named certain areas after Benji. The park itself is not a place of healing for me, but on that particular day at the park, the Lord brought me freedom that I cannot explain. It is not freedom from pain, or from the evil that we suffered. It is the freedom to extend God-given grace to someone whom I had no intention ever to speak kindly to.

There are many who suffer loss and tragedy and carry wounds that cannot be healed because they will not allow the Lord to cut the chain of unforgiveness from their soul. The result is that they are chained to their past in a painful and negative way. They are bitter, and they want others to pay for the injustice they have suffered. If the Lord places an opportunity before you to experience the freedom of forgiveness, take it. Allow Him to break you out of the jail you are in and give you the freedom to walk forward in life.

I return to the words of Joseph for guidance. Notice in the verses at the beginning of this chapter that Joseph was able to be forgiving by not putting himself in the seat of the judge. He was not in the place of God. He was not going to bring justice to bear on the injustice he had suffered. He had a God-centered worldview and recognized that God had brought him to his position in order to be a savior of his family — not a judge who would bring more (and perhaps well-deserved) harm. He also did not forgive by forgetting the past. He said, "What you meant for evil." In other words, "I still know what you did. I still remember how it felt, weeping in that hole, while you talked about whether to sell me or kill me." However, remembering the tragedy does not mean you can't forgive. Joseph went on to say that he would take care of their "little ones." Joseph was choosing to forgive for God's glory and his family's best.

In the same way, we are forgiven by Christ. Romans 5:8 says, "But God demonstrates His own love toward us, in that while we were still sinners, Christ died for us." Choosing to forgive is to choose to be like Christ, understanding that we are forgiven rebels. By God's power, the Lord can use that to save us from years of bitterness and save others through the power of the gospel.

For me, the Lord had to bring me face to face with the person I had held in so much contempt, the person I blamed the most when I remembered the creek bank and the images. Maybe the Lord will not have to do that for you to bring you to that healing place. But, whatever it takes, and whenever the Lord touches your heart and exposes that bitter unforgiveness within your soul, do not let it pass. Take the opportunity to let Him cut the chains that leave you in the tragedy. You will see God's power in ways you never thought possible.

GIVING HIM TO A GREATER FATHER

He said about Benjamin: The Lord's beloved rests securely on Him. He shields him all day long, and he rests on His shoulders. (Deuteronomy 33:12, Holman Christian Standard Bible)

Let not your heart be troubled; you believe in God, believe also in Me. In My Father's house are many mansions; if it were not so, I would have told you. I go to prepare a place for you. And if I go and prepare a place for you, I will come again and receive you to Myself; that where I am, there you may be also. (John 14:1-3)

This is the text we placed on Benji's gravestone. Above it is a picture of him in bed one night after he was saved, holding a Bible. Another picture shows him with a big smile, wearing his Mickey Mouse ears on the Disney trip in 2010. The smiles in those pictures are what we long to remember.

I go from time to time to clean off the grave marker and cut the grass around it. I still feel obligated to say, "I am sorry, buddy, that I did not see and do something that day." I have admitted that to my family and others through the years and have been told that I should not say or think that. I cannot look at my smiling face in that photo taken four minutes before the train accident without thinking I should have noticed something that day. Maybe I should have noticed the speed of the train before ours or the lack of attention to safety by the driver. But I didn't notice anything until it was too late.

On a cold winter day in February 2012, I walked around the railings of the closed Cleveland Park to where it all happened, and I stood with tears in my eyes, feeling once again the crushing weight of failure. It was the feeling of failure to protect my family and others that day. That feeling has followed me for years.

I knew then that I could not control everything or protect my children from all dangers, but the reality can be a crushing weight. It is a major source of prayer and a test of my faith even now. In order to be free of this weight, I must give Benji to a greater Father who prepared a place for him. I must trust my Lord to help me be a father to Seth, Matthew, and Hannah, with the realization that I am not perfect and cannot foresee or protect them from everything.

There is a picture on my phone from the Disney trip. It is a photo of Benji on my shoulders. He is resting his head on my head, and his little chubby fingers are around my chin. I still can remember what it felt like for his hot hands to be wrapped around my chin that day. It was 96 degrees, and I had lifted him up to give him a rest while we watched the Star Wars parade pass by.

My role as a parent has changed since then. I am the dad of a student and firefighter, a 190-pound high school football player, and an eight-year-old princess. All of them need different things from me. I try to carry them on my shoulders in different ways, but I still realize I am limited. I know I must put them in the Lord's hands and trust Him. I must trust my precious wife to the Lord daily and do my best to fulfill my calling as a husband. It is a test of faith that is day-to-day.

I know Benji is resting in the arms of his heavenly Father now. I witnessed his faith and testimony, and I know he loved and trusted the Lord. I still say I am sorry when I am at the grave. I still feel the sting of what I didn't see or could not do that day. In God's sovereign plan, He saw fit to gather Benji to Himself on March 19, 2011. Now he rests securely on God's shoulders.

One of the greatest tests of faith we will face after tragedy and loss is trusting the Lord's sovereign plan and our own weakness. When we accept both, we come before the Lord as Job did in chapter 42:1-3: "Then Job answered the Lord and said: 'I know that You can do everything, And that no purpose of Yours can be withheld from You. You asked, "Who is this who hides counsel without knowledge?" Therefore I have uttered what I did not understand, things too wonderful for me, which I did not know.'"

THE TEARS OF JESUS

Therefore, when Jesus saw her weeping, and the Jews who came with her weeping, He groaned in the spirit and was troubled. And He said, "Where have you laid him?" They said to Him, "Lord, come and see." Jesus wept. Then the Jews said, "See how He loved him!" (John 11:33-36)

Then was fulfilled what was spoken by Jeremiah the prophet, saying: "A voice was heard in Ramah, lamentation, weeping, and great mourning, Rachel weeping for her children, refusing to be comforted, because they are no more." (Matthew 2:17-18)

One of the most difficult things to navigate in marriage has to be the death of a child. My wife and I learned very quickly that we grieve differently. A lot of decisions became challenges to our emotions and feelings. How much space to give your wife? How do you talk about the unspeakable? How do you avoid saying the wrong things? How do you support your wife, and how does she support you as you try to recover your life?

I still remember Tabitha lying on the bed feeding Hannah, reading her Bible and praying — and crying. She told me, "I wonder if this baby will ever talk. All I do is cry."

One day a pastor friend came by to take me to lunch. As we rode around, he asked me if he could do anything for me. That question broke me instantly. My eyes filled up with tears, and I said something like, "Just ride me around a little. Tabitha doesn't need to see me crying."

For me, seeing her crying and trying to be strong was more than I could take. She would talk about wanting to hear Benji again, or feel his soft face and his hair. As a firefighter for twenty-nine years, I have told Tabitha many times that the worst thing for me was hearing a mother's cry when her baby was dead. It was terrible when I didn't know the person, but it is horrifying as a husband when you can't fix it. To this day, I cannot read Matthew 2 without choking up. The reality of mothers wailing and the words "no more" are pressure points on my very soul. I cannot praise the Lord enough for His strength and the extraordinary faith of my wife through her journey of grief.

Today we still hurt, but we can talk of the memories, both good and bad. We still shed tears together on special days and at the grave, and that is all right. I have been made better by my wife and her journey in grief and faith. Her daily walk with the Lord has greatly influenced our children to trust the Lord when they are hurting and do not have the answers. It is a hard journey together, but the Lord has given us grace to help one another.

As we journey on this pathway of grief, we have the hope of heaven, but also the peace and security that the Lord is here, walking with us in this journey on the earth. John 11 teaches us that Jesus could not only raise the dead, but that He could also sympathize with our weakness. He could sit with the brokenhearted and weep with them. We can be sustained in the days to come knowing that Jesus knows our sorry and weeps with us as we suffer in a fallen world. We trust that Benji is in heaven, and we trust, through Jesus, that we will join him one day.

But we also know we will never hear his footsteps again, feel his face, see him hug his sister, or play sports in school. We weep for the "no more," the things we cannot change and the things that we will miss. Yet, in our tears, we do not look to a stone-faced Savior. We look into the face of a Savior with tear stains on His face. He is a Savior who is acquainted with sorrow and grief and ready to walk with us through this journey.

Are you weeping for what is no more? Take it to the Savior today. He understands your tears.

THE MESSENGER

"The Spirit of the Lord God is upon Me, Because the Lord has anointed Me to preach good tidings to the poor; He has sent Me to heal the brokenhearted, to proclaim liberty to the captives, and the opening of the prison to those who are bound; to proclaim the acceptable year of the Lord, and the day of vengeance of our God; to comfort all who mourn, to console those who mourn in Zion, to give them beauty for ashes, the oil of joy for mourning, the garment of praise for the spirit of heaviness; that they may be called trees of righteousness, the planting of the Lord, that He may be glorified." (Isaiah 61:1-3)

I was rushed into a trauma room in Spartanburg Regional Medical Center with a large gash in my head and my foot turned sideways. I was strapped down to a backboard. (I had done that many times to people as a firefighter, "packaging them for transport.") I don't remember much about the pain while I was rolled in. I saw the lights and ceiling tiles go by and wondered what part of the emergency area was I going to. I was trying to think of where everyone else might be.

Doctors and nurses were rushing around me and examining my injuries. Meds and tests were quickly ordered. After a while, the traffic slowed, but I was still on the backboard for precautionary reasons as they cleaned my wounds in my head and prepared to take me for tests. I had heard nothing from anyone about the kids, and only that Tabitha was having some pains and was getting checked out. I knew what I saw in that park, and I knew it would have to be a miracle for Benji to survive. I was crying and praying that the Lord would help us.

A nurse came in to work on my head. I do not recall seeing her face. I only saw her scrubs from the corner of my eye, and when she leaned over, I saw a blonde curl beside my face. She spoke softly and asked me if I was crying because of my pain. She offered to get me some meds. I told her I believed my son had died and I didn't know what to do. She told me her parents were missionaries, and she asked me if she could share some Scripture with me. I told her, "Yes, please." She quoted Isaiah 61 and prayed for my broken heart to be healed and for me to know that the Lord is close to the brokenhearted. She prayed that the Lord would let me see beauty in the ashes. I don't remember seeing or hearing her again. Shortly after that, Tabitha was brought in with a hospital representative to tell me that Benji had died.

I will never forget what the Lord did through His servant that day. That young lady who helped me was a messenger of God's truth to my soul — right before I was told that my son had died. The passage from Isaiah was familiar to me, but after that it became a core Scripture in my life. I requested that it be read at Benji's funeral, and it has been a passage that I have preached from several times to share God's comfort to those who mourn.

In the months after the accident, I began to engage and witness to an older gentleman who was not a believer but was open to hearing the gospel. He struggled with pain, depression and anger in his life. I thought I could help him, and he seemed willing to hear me out. On one occasion, however, he became belligerent and asked, "Where was God when your son was killed? How can you believe in a God like that?" He stormed out of my office and, quite honestly, left me reeling in despair. I didn't have an answer for why God would allow that to happen. I believed God was there, but that didn't mean I understood it. I was left with God's silence instead of answers.

In his book *When Heaven Is Silent,* Ron Dunn says that "the silence of God is suspicious. Like a witness who pleads the fifth, God's silence is interpreted as a guilty silence. For Job, the question was no longer his innocence, but God's innocence. … And so Job indicts God. He determines the questions to be answered. He demands that God justify His actions. He is never informed of the conversation in heaven between God and Satan. … There are many wounded people that will live their days and die without knowing why tragedy interrupted their lives. If only God would say something. All I am asking for is some clue as to why all these things happened. … But like Job, we learn the tough lesson that God is not obligated to explain His actions. Humans need a system of justice, God does not. … In the end God tells Job only this truth: He has a right to do what He does. God alone, who has created the universe, has the right to govern and the right to say whether He is governing it properly."

In my despair, and in the silence, I thought of those verses from Isaiah and the prayer of the nurse that day in the hospital. I recalled that those verses were read by Jesus in the synagogue of Nazareth. Jesus said the words were being fulfilled in His listeners' ears because He was the fulfillment of the words.

Jesus did not come to a human race that already had all the answers. We have no answers. We suffer, we die, and we hurt. We are brokenhearted now, or we soon will be. That is precisely why we need a Savior. He is someone who can reverse the curse and bring beauty from the ashes and healing to those who mourn. I can know, as Dunn says, that God has a right to do what He does. At the same time, I know that He is the answer to my greatest need. He intervened in grace to heal our brokenness and to show us how He can bring about good in a fallen world.

Hebrews 1:1-2 says, "God, who at various times and in various ways spoke in times past to the fathers by the prophets, has in these last days spoken to us by His Son, whom He has appointed heir of all things, through whom also He made the worlds." Jesus has revealed a new way. Although both the righteous and the wicked suffer in a fallen world, only one has the promise of beauty in the ashes. Only the believer has the promise of comfort in his or her mourning and healing for a broken heart.

We weep at the grave, yet our hearts are lifted to our Savior in hope. Like those listeners in Nazareth who heard Jesus read the words of Isaiah 61, we also have a choice: to look to Him, or to continue on a path that leads to further heartache. For me, these verses are proof of God's power to speak to my heart when I need it most, and they are an anchor to my soul when the devils rage and ask, "Where is your God?"

It reminds me of the words of Henry Wadsworth Longfellow in "I Heard the Bells on Christmas Day." He wrote the words in 1863 in the midst of the Civil War while nursing his injured son back to health. He reached a point nearing despair as he heard the Christmas bells in the church tower and could see no end to the war raging in his nation. He wrote: "And in despair I bowed my head. There is no peace on earth, I said; for hate is strong, and mocks the song of peace on earth good will to men."

This is a point we all eventually reach, because we live in a fallen world with all of its unanswered questions. Where do we go from there? Do we stay there in the pit of despair?

But hear the words of Longfellow, as he transitions to what he knows by faith: "Then pealed the bells more loud and deep: God is not dead, nor doth He sleep; The wrong shall fail, the Right prevail, with peace on earth, good will to men."

This is the faith of Isaiah 61 and Luke 4. We trust in a Savior who came to us in our brokenness and is bringing healing and comfort through a new and better kingdom through His blood.

I have considered many times the work of the Lord through that nurse, and how we should put more stock in God's Word and less stock in our pithy sayings when someone is grieving or hurting. There is more value in the Scriptures than in the words we stumble over while trying to say something helpful.

When I am hurting, I really do not need someone telling me that my child is another rose in God's garden, or that he is an angel in heaven now, or that God has His reasons. I do not need to be told that God wanted him more or that only the good die young. I need to know that a mighty Savior came to this earth to heal the brokenhearted, and He is working to bring beauty to the ashes of my life in ways that I cannot see or know.

Let us never stop looking to the Savior or pointing people to Him when they are in their darkest moments.

Forced into the Boat

And when the disciples saw Him walking on the sea, they were troubled, saying, "It is a ghost!" And they cried out for fear. But immediately Jesus spoke to them, saying, "Be of good cheer! It is I; do not be afraid." And Peter answered Him and said, "Lord, if it is You, command me to come to You on the water." So He said, "Come." And when Peter had come down out of the boat, he walked on the water to go to Jesus. (Matthew 14:26-29)

"I always thought of faith as a buffer, a cushion that would protect me from the sharp edges of life. When one of those edges pierced my flesh and penetrated my flesh — that is when the questions began. That is when I made the shattering discovery: You can trust God and still get hurt." (Ron Dunn, When Heaven Is Silent)

When I read these words by Ron Dunn, I thought of how blessed and easy my life had been up to that point. I was born premature, weighing only three pounds. It was a life-changing experience for my mom and dad. They had waited fifteen years to have a child, and when I was born it was a life-threatening situation, with my being that small.

I grew up being told that God had worked a miracle to save my life and that my parents had given their lives over to the Lord after those long, grueling months in the hospital. Our family life was not always the easiest, but I was sheltered and given the best they could give. I was taught to go further than my mom and dad had gone in life and to value God's calling and education. The church I was blessed to grow up in gave me the gospel, my understanding of the Scriptures, and my wife.

Our life together as a married couple was blessed, and our children were the fulfillment of our dreams. I had pastored two churches and had been blessed with seeing positive change in both. The churches God had given me to lead became our family and friends. Truly, my life was evidence of God's goodness and power.

Then, out of the blue, the storm hit my life and took away my security and peace. Matthew 14 describes a storm that must have given the disciples a similar feeling. They had just witnessed a great miracle, the feeding of the 5,000. However, at the end of this miraculous event, Jesus made them get into a boat and go to the other side.

The disciples no doubt were baffled by the sudden pressure that Jesus placed upon them to leave the area. John records why Jesus was making them leave: "Therefore when Jesus perceived that they were about to come and take Him by force to make Him king, He departed again to the mountain by Himself alone. Now when evening came, His disciples went down to the sea, got into the boat, and went over the sea toward Capernaum. And it was already dark, and Jesus had not come to them" (John 6:15-17). The Lord was taking them out of this high point to protect them from what they could not see coming.

The result of the forced removal from this great moment was a storm. This terrifying and life-threatening moment seems out of place in the context of events, but when we see it for what it says, it can help us through the storms of life. For Jesus, there was as much danger in leaving the disciples with a fickle crowd as there was in putting them in the midst of a storm that threatened their lives.

There is a certain danger in success and ease that can be far more destructive than sudden life-threatening moments. Satan uses success and ease to lure us into things that can pull us away from God's purpose. Jesus withdrew from the crowd, but He knew His disciples would be left there with baskets full of bread, to be bombarded by the opinions of a crowd that would want their bellies full tomorrow. So He put them into a boat heading straight into a storm.

At three o'clock in the morning, the disciples had all but forgotten the miracle of the previous day and were fighting for their lives. They were about four miles out, almost halfway across the Sea of Galilee, before Jesus walked toward them on the water. They were terrified. However, a great lesson was about to be learned in the crisis.

Peter looked around and, seeing Jesus, asked Jesus to command him to come to Him on the water. Peter stepped out on the water and walked toward Jesus. There is a moment in a crisis when the believer must decide who and what he can trust in the storm. Can he trust the man-made answers he has used to navigate through life for so long, or does he abandon those things and simply say to Jesus, "Lord if it is you, let me come to you!"

The disciples learned this in success and in the storm. Whatever circumstances we face, it is better to look to the Lord than try to deal with it on our own. Peter became overwhelmed by the waves before him and cried out to Jesus to save him. Jesus stretched forth His hand and took hold of Peter and walked to the boat. John records that when Jesus stepped into the boat, it was immediately on the other side. The disciples were led away from the disaster of following the whims of a fickle crowd and away from their own ideas of the ease and comfort that success could bring. The Lord permitted the storm and the grief that followed in those gut-wrenching hours to protect them from what they could not see.

Returning to those great lessons I learned through the life of Joseph,

I find in this story the security of knowing that whatever the Lord allows, good or bad, it can be used for our good. We praise the Lord for the storms. We praise Him for the opportunity to see His power and walk with Him on the water. We praise Him for the opportunity to see how our answers and our ideas are not sufficient for what we face in life. We are driven to the Savior, and we learn in good times and bad that He is the answer to our deepest needs. In the storm, the Savior is further revealed. The power of God is made known in a way that we would not have so easily recognized until our attention was completely placed upon Him coming along on the water. Like Peter, we see in the storm His power over nature and circumstances, His purposes, our insufficiency, and the peace of walking with Jesus, who is holding up our arms.

My parents are getting older and have experienced some major health issues. At times, they have been unsteady while walking and have required assistance. My mom will often get up and reach for my arm to feel secure. I often think of how life works like that. When we are young, our life gravitates toward security and stability; and when we are old, we still look for those things. It seems when we are in our prime we forget that we still need security and stability. We begin to imagine that we have things all taken care of and we can handle what life throws at us.

We need to be reminded of what Solomon said in Ecclesiastes 12:1-4: "Remember now your Creator in the days of your youth, before the difficult days come, and the years draw near when you say, 'I have no pleasure in them'; while the sun and the light, the moon and the stars, are not darkened, and the clouds do not return after the rain; in the day when the keepers of the house tremble, and the strong men bow down; when the grinders cease because they are few, and those that look through the windows grow dim; when the doors are shut in the streets, and the sound of grinding is low; when one rises up at the sound of a bird, and all the daughters of music are brought low."

These reminders are not easy to learn when everything is going well, when we feel strong enough to handle whatever comes our way. However, there are things that are coming our way we cannot handle. We all need, in our prime, to see the Savior who can feed the 5,000, the Savior who can calm the storm at three in the morning. Both lessons are needed to remember our Creator, while we are young.

I realize, at forty-six years old, that there will be more storms to come. I am thankful I can look back on the worst day of my life and say that the Lord came to me on the water. He has shown me, in the darkest moment, what I needed to know about Him. He is the God who is with us in the storm, and He is not affected in the least by what is life-threatening to us. He is the eternal, all powerful, gracious Savior who bids us leave our little bashed boats and walk to Him. He is the One who can take us where we need to be after we have fought all our lives to only go halfway.

This knowledge of the Savior does not come from ease; it comes from the storm. The fear of God and the submission to His sovereign will does not come from success; it only comes from reaching the end of ourselves and, in desperation, crying out to Him. There is one thing I am continually aware of now more than I was before Benji's death: my own desperate fragility. I find myself crying out to the Lord in my spirit for help now more than I did then. I call out to my Savior to keep me from the things that I cannot see that can destroy my effectiveness as His disciple.

I am terrified not of death, but of what success can do to me, and of what the storm can do if I try to stay inside my little man-made boat of answers. I need the Savior to find me at 3:00 a.m. when I cannot find myself.

I also need to know the purpose in the pain. I cannot go on in this fallen world if the storms of grief, depression and suffering are meaningless. I need to see the purpose, as the disciples did. After the storm, they saw the purpose. They were able to say afterward, in Matthew 14:33, "Truly You are the Son of God." They worshipped and glorified Him after the storm because they knew Him more intimately.

They also knew their own limitations intimately. I am thankful there is purpose in the pain. It is the purpose that Paul celebrated when he said, in 2 Corinthians 12:8-9, "Concerning this thing I pleaded with the Lord three times that it might depart from me. And He said to me, 'My grace is sufficient for you, for My strength is made perfect in weakness.' Therefore most gladly I will rather boast in my infirmities, that the power of Christ may rest upon me."

Also, Paul said to Timothy: "For this reason I also suffer these things; nevertheless I am not ashamed, for I know whom I have believed and am persuaded that He is able to keep what I have committed to Him until that Day" (2 Timothy 1:12).

The purpose in the storm is what we hold on to going forward. Each day, I try to leave behind the images and the depressing negativity and fatalism that carries me back to the images of the horror of March 19, 2011, but the only way to really leave it behind is to hold on to the Savior who taught me His purposes through that pain. I still remember the pain — the waves. I still remember the desperation and panic of those days and the darkness in my soul in the months that followed. I will not forget those painful things, but I also remember the kindness of the Savior who stretched forth His hands at my three a.m. moment.

The arms of Jesus sustain my children in their faith and lift up my wife to smile again, and help me as a pastor to continue to lead a church and preach when my soul seems too dark to see which way was up. The powerful hands of the Savior sustain me and give me the ability to keep believing, preaching, and serving even when the waves are too big for me. They help me speak confidently to people in their darkest moments, knowing that I did not feel confident enough in myself to say those things, or even pray. The power of God has kept me going when I sat alone wanting to quit, feeling I had failed as a leader — and really not wanting my kids, my wife, or my church family to know that I couldn't take it any longer. This power of God was not realized in the successful years of blessings and ease. It was realized in the terrifying realities of the storm and its aftermath.

A dear friend, speaking about the loss of his precious wife of fifty-two years, said, "I am not sure I ever want to 'get over it.'" I do not want to get over what I learned in this storm, because it has changed me, and I am fearful of what would happen if these lessons were not in my life now.

More storms (and more successes) may be on the horizon for me, and they may be on your horizon, also. We can know that whatever comes our way, it is best to be with Jesus even if He has forced us into a storm.

PERMITTING YOURSELF TO MOVE FORWARD

The Lord knows the thoughts of man, that they are futile. Blessed is the man whom You instruct, O Lord, and teach out of Your law, that You may give him rest from the days of adversity, until the pit is dug for the wicked. (Psalm 94:11-13)

David therefore pleaded with God for the child, and David fasted and went in and lay all night on the ground. So the elders of his house arose and went to him, to raise him up from the ground. But he would not, nor did he eat food with them. Then on the seventh day it came to pass that the child died. And the servants of David were afraid to tell him that the child was dead. For they said, "Indeed, while the child was alive, we spoke to him, and he would not heed our voice. How can we tell him that the child is dead? He may do some harm!" When David saw that his servants were whispering, David perceived that the child was dead. Therefore David said to his servants, "Is the child dead?" And they said, "He is dead." So David arose from the ground, washed and anointed himself, and changed his clothes; and he went into the house of the Lord and worshiped. Then he went to his own house; and when he requested, they set food before him, and he ate. Then his servants said to him, "What is this that you have done? You fasted and wept for the child while he was alive, but when the child died, you arose and ate food." And he said, "While the child was alive, I fasted and wept; for I said, 'Who can tell whether the Lord will be gracious to me, that the child may live?' But now he is dead; why should I fast? Can I bring him back again? I shall go to him, but he shall not return to me." (2 Samuel 12:16-23)

But I do not want you to be ignorant, brethren, concerning those who have fallen asleep, lest you sorrow as others who have no hope. For if we believe that Jesus died and rose again, even so God will bring with Him those who sleep in Jesus. For this we say to you by the word of the Lord, that we who are alive and remain until the coming of the Lord will by no means precede those who are asleep. For the Lord Himself will descend from heaven with a shout, with the voice of an archangel, and with the trumpet of God. And the dead in Christ will rise first. Then we who are alive and remain shall be caught up together with them in the clouds to meet the Lord in the air. And thus we shall always be with the Lord. Therefore comfort one another with these words. (1 Thessalonians 4:13-18)

One of the biggest challenges in my grief was to allow myself to move forward. A part of me still struggles with allowing myself to be happy or be motivated again.

I remember in the months after the accident looking out the window and seeing Tabitha's car parked at the cemetery after taking the kids to school. I remember watching the kids walk into school and not seeing Benji sleepily following after. There were joys and happy times during those months, and there was laughter. But there was also the sting of guilt for even smiling.

I remember reading the account of David when his baby died and being encouraged by his faith and his ability to move forward in his grief, but I didn't know how we were going to do that. Those were hard days of grief. Often I became emotional laughing with friends because I felt I was betraying Benji by enjoying myself. I wanted my kids and Tabitha to have joy and happiness again, but deep down I didn't know how to do that without feeling guilty.

After some months, I noticed Tabitha didn't go to the grave as often. She would still shed tears and talk about Benji and the things she missed about him, but stopping by the grave was less frequent. Then I overheard her say, "I know Benji would not want me to feel guilt over this. He loved his momma too much. So I don't feel like I have to go by there all the time." That was a freeing moment for her.

For me, it wasn't so much the grave; it was just allowing myself to enjoy life and what the Lord had left me. I had to focus on two things to move forward. First, I had to focus on what I believed about heaven and the reality that Benji was experiencing — that being absent from the body meant he was present with the Lord. He was okay — and even more than okay. He was better than he was before. He was at peace with the Savior he loved.

The torture I inflicted on myself because he was gone from this earth did not help him or me. By faith I had to say, like David, that I could go to him, but he could not come back — and he wouldn't want to, anyway. The reality of the resurrection is the source of comfort that can get us through these psychological wars that come from the process of grief.

Paul's audience in 1 Thessalonians was struggling with the idea that their deceased loved ones who trusted Christ were going to miss out on the resurrection. This caused them grief, sadness and maybe even guilt as they looked toward the second coming. Paul's words were given to them to resolve the grief that comes from ignorance. Those who sleep are not at a disadvantage. On the contrary, they are at a great advantage because they will be the first to be given their glorified body and we will rise in the air to meet Jesus at the sound of the last trumpet.

For the believer who is grieving over the death of another believer, we do not grieve as those who have no hope. We grieve with hope. We understand what we and the world lost when our loved one passed from this life, but we know also what our loved one has gained. As Paul says in Romans 8:18, "For I consider that the sufferings of this present time are not worthy to be compared with the glory which shall be revealed in us." The glory they are experiencing is beyond our imagination. Because of this, we grieve in hope and look toward the skies.

I have often sat beside the elderly as they were dying and listened to them talk about those who have gone on before them and who they hoped to see with Jesus. They miss their parents, their spouse, and their children who have gone ahead to glory, but they look to Jesus and to the reality that those in Christ are with them. In this way, the physical death of a loved one is only one more reason to look toward the glory to come instead of a despair that destroys our hope.

I cannot talk in this manner without thinking of those who have suffered through the pain of a loved one passing from this earth. The pain must be especially intense for those who do not know the eternal state of their loved ones. The Scripture leaves no loophole or middle ground. Heaven or hell is the final destination. This should be a great motivation to us to share the gospel with those in our families and make sure, as the old song says, that the circle remains unbroken. There is a special place in my heart for the parent who must bury a teenage or adult child without knowing if they ever trusted Jesus. If that is you, then know that the Lord is a God of comfort who knows your tears.

Benji's gravesite has one of the most beautiful yet incidental qualities. Many clouds come from the south toward Gaffney, South Carolina. In the evenings, as these clouds approach after a rain, a person can stand in our church parking lot and see beautiful rainbows. The rainbows sometimes line up directly over Benji's grave and the graves of four of the precious children of church members who have passed since his death.

We would never have had the insight or the forethought to plan it that way, but each rainbow reminds me of two wonderful things. I am reminded of Benji's rainbow drawing from kindergarten, which sits on our dresser, and I am reminded of the great promise that one day the Lord will appear in the eastern sky, and the dead in Christ will rise first. When we meet Jesus in the air on that day, we will see that our loved ones are already there and have their promises fulfilled in a glorified body. With this hope, we rise up and move forward.

We cannot move forward without hope, and we cannot move forward without purpose. Why did David get up and wash himself and regain his strength? He had an understanding that the Lord was not finished with him yet.

I believe the Lord refilled our lives with purpose through Seth, Matthew and Hannah. Hannah was born April 27, 2011, a little more than a month after the train accident. Looking back, it becomes quickly evident that Hannah was sent to us as a comfort and as a challenge for us to get moving.

I remember speaking with a counselor friend about Seth and Matthew. I was worried about what they were living with and what they weren't saying. She plainly told me, "They will probably do better than you. Children have a simple faith in the Lord." Over time, I saw that she was right. The boys immediately regained their big brother modes, only this time with a protector mindset over their little sister. I watch Hannah now, at eight years old, with her brothers, and I see how the Lord helped the boys move forward by giving them a cuddly sweet little blonde sister with a gentle spirit.

The aftermath of David's adultery with Bathsheba is a tragic story of more grief and pain for him. However, I have thought many times that what kept David going was his role in the kingdom work of the Lord and in his son. He said, "Now, my son, may the Lord be with you; and may you prosper, and build the house of the Lord your God, as He has said to you. Only may the Lord give you wisdom and understanding, and give you charge concerning Israel, that you may keep the law of the Lord your God" (1 Chronicles 22:11-12).

Like David, I have found the kingdom work of God and my family to be the purpose in my pain. Watching the Lord work in my children has proven to be what the Lord has used to keep me going. Also, seeing lives changed with the gospel of Jesus has kept me from being enveloped in negativity and purposelessness.

Bill Poore came to my house several weeks after the accident and told me he believed that it would soon be time for me to return to the pulpit. This advice was for me as well as the church family that was grieving with me. To get back to the pulpit required that I consider the Lord's will and His people.

Bill was right. Getting back to the work of preaching focused me on eternity and on kingdom initiatives. It also gave me motivation to minister to the hurting people who had stopped their own lives in order to help us. To remain down, reliving the accident, brought me continued despair. To be challenged by God's Word forced me out of the past and into the future. It gave me an opportunity to be transparent with others and to vocalize my faith even when I struggled emotionally and psychologically with the present realities.

Moving forward does not mean we forget the past. It means we accept what cannot be changed, and we get moving to join the Lord in

His work, knowing that He is the only One who can give us hope and purpose in the darkest hours.

When I think of 1 Thessalonians 4, I cannot help but remember the role of the church in grief. I have told people, with tears in my eyes, that the biggest challenge to my ever leaving Corinth Baptist Church is the thought of leaving my church family. There are people I could never repay for what they have done for me and my family.

One of those church family members was a deacon who sat on my porch after the train accident and shared with me how his parents had died at a young age. Later in life, he was drafted into military service in Vietnam and found himself in the jungle asking God why He had sent him through so much hell. As he spoke of the hardships, the discussion shifted to how the Lord used that experience to bring him to salvation when he returned from the war. The transparency of that faith discussion was a powerful help to me.

I will never forget the deacons of the church carrying Benji's casket to the gravesite, or the book some members had printed with pictures and with church members' "Benji Stories" in it. I will never forget the tears of Benji's babysitters and Sunday school teachers and the special things they did to honor him.

I will never forget how a faithful older couple cut the grass over his grave until they could no longer physically do so. I will never forget how the youth group placed glass over Benji's name on the youth room board to protect it from ever being erased, and how that signature was copied and made into stickers for us and church members to place on our cars and personal items. I won't forget the thousands of dollars raised by the church and community to build a playground in memory of Benji.

These things are just a few examples of the love poured out on us — just through our church — in our grief. That does not even include the letters, calls, hugs, and prayers of untold thousands of believers. The believer's bond to the church is a lifeline of comfort and help. I know I could not have made it through these years with any semblance of health without the church.

When a believer is going through grief and loss, the tendency many times is to isolate himself and seek distance from people. However, I have found that the key to picking up the pieces of your life and finding purpose again is to be with the people of the Lord. With God's people, we find examples of endurance and testimonies of God's strength and power. With God's people, we find others who also hurt with hope.

I have spoken to people on multiple occasions who have told me that after their loved one died, they just could not return to worship with the church. They felt it would cause too much pain or be too difficult. I completely understand this, but this thought process is actually very destructive for the believer. Not only do we remove ourselves from the Lord's ministry to us through others, but we also remove a big part of our testimony that could lead others to Christ.

We as a family, by being a part of the church through the years, have seen how the Lord was faithful to so many who have suffered great loss. We have learned through the testimony of others how to have hope in grief. For this and many other things, I am eternally grateful for the blessing of the saints.

THE RAINBOW AROUND THE THRONE

After these things I looked, and behold, a door standing open in heaven. And the first voice which I heard was like a trumpet speaking with me, saying, "Come up here, and I will show you things which must take place after this." Immediately I was in the Spirit; and behold, a throne set in heaven, and One sat on the throne. And He who sat there was like a jasper and a sardius stone in appearance; and there was a rainbow around the throne, in appearance like an emerald. (Revelation 4:1-3)

I saw still another mighty angel coming down from heaven, clothed with a cloud. And a rainbow was on his head, his face was like the sun, and his feet like pillars of fire. (Revelation 10:1)

For now we see in a mirror, dimly, but then face to face. Now I know in part, but then I shall know just as I also am known. (1 Corinthians 13:12)

In August of 2011, I was in physical rehabilitation for the dislocated ankle I had suffered in the train accident. Several times per week, I was traveling to Spartanburg for rehabilitation. During these trips, Adrian Rogers' sermons would be playing on the radio. On one particular occasion, his sermon radically changed me in my grief.

He was preaching on Revelation 4 and the throne room of God. As he explained the text, he stated that scientists tell us that, standing on the earth, we only see half of the rainbow because of the horizon. However, looking from above the earth, one can see that the rainbow is a complete circle. When I heard this, my heart jumped with joy. He said the vision of John shows those who see the throne in heaven do not see God's promises half-filled, they see God's promises complete in His power and sovereignty.

As a grieving parent, much of my thought processes gravitate toward what Benji has been missing. How he missed the birth of his sister. How he missed elementary school or his brother Seth graduating from high school. How he missed following in Matthew's and Seth's footsteps in middle school or seeing Seth play the drums or watching his brother Matthew play varsity football.

When I see Hannah being tickled by her big brothers and hear her squeal, I always think about how Benji would have loved that squeal. I think about how he will miss that first girlfriend, or having a family with kids who act like him.

It is like losing some of your future to think about what your child has missed. What would he have looked like as a young teenager? Would he have been big and muscular, or tall and skinny? Would school come easy, or would he struggle with grades? What would life have been like if he were still here?

All these things have left me empty many times through the years, but I always return to that sermon by Adrian Rogers and the tears I shed in victory that morning while driving to rehabilitation. The Lord gave me a spiritual shot to my soul, which was needed to cure the hopelessness caused by unanswered questions and unfulfilled dreams.

The cure was the knowledge that there are no unfulfilled dreams and unanswered questions before the throne. There is no one before God's throne right now worshiping the Lamb who sees only partial fulfillments of God's promises. They see what the Lord was doing in His divine sovereignty and in His timing. They are not hindered by life under the sun, as Solomon describes it. The saints of God who have gone on before us see the purpose in their pain. They see why their lives were limited to the years they had on this earth. They know what the Lord was doing when He called them home. Those in heaven understand what they were saved from and who was brought to salvation through their lives or their deaths.

We are not yet privy to such knowledge as believers. We only see a partial rainbow. Just like Stephen, as he was being stoned, did not know that Saul was watching when he looked to see the Savior standing at the right hand of God, we do not know if our life or even our death will help bring a Saul to salvation.

The last school drawing made by Benji became even more important to me after hearing this sermon. It was a drawing of a rainbow, but a partial and shortened rainbow, with Benji riding on a unicorn on top of it. I remember looking at that drawing when it was found in Benji's school bag and thinking that the partial rainbow spoke volumes about a life of promise cut short. It spoke to my unfulfilled dreams for my son and the loss of our future together. All the "no mores" flooded my soul.

However, the message of Revelation 4 is a clear and powerful reinforcement that these thoughts, however valid on this earth, are illegitimate in heaven. As Paul says in 1 Corinthians 13:12, "For now we see in a mirror, dimly, but then face to face. Now I know in part, but then I shall know just as I also am known." At this moment, we see through a mirror dimly, and we see a partial rainbow on the horizon, but one day all of that will be corrected.

As a parent, I miss seeing all of the things that could have been, and

I still grieve for those things. However, by faith, I can celebrate the truth that my son is not before God's throne worried about what could have been or why something happened. He knows, as he is known. He sees clearly the things that are beyond my visual range. He has answers to questions that still nag my soul in this fallen world. I peer into a dim mirror and have to trust that the Lord is working for good. I can't see the other end of the rainbow, but I have to believe that God's promise is going to be fulfilled. Benji is experiencing perfect reality, and I am still living by faith.

Walking by faith means that we do not walk by sight. I remember that one of the first Facebook posts about Benji said, "Gone but not forgotten." I appreciated every act of love and every comforting message we received, but the word "gone" stuck in my mind as a torturous word. Another phrase in the news media was "taken too soon."

These phrases, which reflect the perspective of this fallen world, are like the statements of Solomon: "He has made everything beautiful in its time. Also He has put eternity in their hearts, except that no one can find out the work that God does from beginning to end" (Ecclesiastes 3:11) or, "I said in my heart, 'Concerning the condition of the sons of men, God tests them, that they may see that they themselves are like animals.' For what happens to the sons of men also happens to animals; one thing befalls them: as one dies, so dies the other. Surely, they all have one breath; man has no advantage over animals, for all is vanity. All go to one place: all are from the dust, and all return to dust" (Ecclesiastes 3:18-20).

This perspective is "under the sun," in the realm of finite minds and limited understanding, where things do not make sense and life is not fair. It is the perspective where people accuse God of not being good or fair, and they shake their fist at heaven and demand that God explain Himself.

However, the message from heaven is always the same. It is the message that the Lord brought to Job: "Then the Lord answered Job out of the whirlwind, and said: 'Now prepare yourself like a man; I will question you, and you shall answer Me: Would you indeed annul My judgment? Would you condemn Me that you may be justified? Have you an arm like God? Or can you thunder with a voice like His?'" (Job 40:6-9).

The message is that we are not God, and we cannot see all He is doing under the sun. We must trust His power, wisdom, and goodness and know that one day before His throne we will see the complete circle of His promises. One day we will see more than a dim reflection; we will see the Savior's face and know that He knew best.

I stake my life and my future upon this truth. If this is not true, then I am destined to a life of bitterness and disappointment. I cannot stand with any more grieving parents or preach any more sermons calling people to trust the Lord. I cannot go on without the rainbow around the throne.

Some days I still stand under the hot sun of this life and wonder if I can go on in a fallen world where things seem so random and out of control, but like on those hot summer days when I was growing up, I return to the water of God's Word and squint to see the rainbow again. I have never failed to see it when I have cried out to the Lord. His Word is faithful. His throne is sure.

THE MULTITUDE OF ANXIETIES

Unless the Lord had been my help, My soul would soon have settled in silence. If I say, "My foot slips," Your mercy, O Lord, will hold me up. In the multitude of my anxieties within me, Your comforts delight my soul. (Psalm 94:17-19)

———————

This past Christmas season we drove to see the Christmas lights at the Charlotte Motor Speedway. When we arrived at the area where activities were going on, I immediately saw an amusement ride and a miniature train. My anxiety level went up as I wondered if Hannah would ask to ride. After the train accident, Seth and Matthew returned to riding amusement rides at Carowinds, but I told them plainly through the years that I no longer felt comfortable with smaller operations because of safety concerns. Hannah looked at me and asked me the question I was hoping she would not: "Daddy, can I ride that?" I watched the perfectly safe-looking miniature train going by and just said, "Not tonight, baby."

It was just too much, and my heart sank with anxiety and guilt because my little girl has to live with that. I no longer live under the assumption that I can shield my children from everything. Many of my prayer times are spent crying out to the Lord to spare my children from the hurt and pain of a fallen world and meditating on the Scriptures that tell us we will suffer in this life. I know they are in the Lord's hands; releasing them to the Lord in this life and giving them the freedom to succeed or fail carries with it a certain kind of anxiety that comes when you know you have already buried a child.

How do we handle this anxiety, or any of the anxieties of life, and keep moving forward? As the psalmist stated, there are a multitude of anxieties. Psalm 94 is a powerful message about anxiety. In the text, the psalmist begins by sharing the sources of anxiety. He knows that God is a God of vengeance, but the psalmist is struggling with why God would let the wicked seemingly prevail so many times. He struggles with the proud boast of the wicked and their horrible actions.

Circumstances that are beyond our control, and the things that people say and do, can greatly hinder our lives if we allow those things to control our thoughts. The psalmist does not have an answer to any of these questions or seeming injustices in his own life. However, that does not hinder him from confessing his faith in the Lord. He confesses what he knows about God — that God is powerful, patient and persistent in His actions. He knows the thoughts of the wicked, He knows the plight of His people, and He will work to set things right.

This is a powerful perspective that can give us the confidence to keep moving forward, even though we do not have all the answers at the moment. The psalmist's position is clarified in Psalm 94:12: "Blessed is the man whom You instruct, O Lord, and teach out of Your law, that You may give him rest from the days of adversity, until the pit is dug for the wicked." We see that the cure for the paralysis of fear is faith and confidence in the Lord. This position of faith does not erase the circumstances around us or the anxiety that we feel about those things, but we give those anxieties to the Lord. Like the psalmist, I can say, "Unless the Lord had been my help, my soul would soon have settled in silence."

I know I could not have made it through many of the dark valleys in my life without the help of the Lord. I can say with the psalmist, "In the multitude of my anxieties within me, Your comforts delight my soul." These statements of faith do not erase the bad memories or the possibilities of bad circumstances and trials of life in the future. However, I can trust Him even when I do not see clearly what God is doing or if I don't have answers to my questions. I can look to Him for comfort in the multitude of my anxieties because He, as a sympathetic High Priest, knows what I am going through and what I need.

A few years ago I went through training in the fire department that was meant to mentally prepare a firefighter for a "Mayday" event and increase the odds of survival in a threatening situation. Some of the situations included wall or floor collapse, and low-air situations that were immediately dangerous to life or health. Many times, the instructors would place things over your mask and blind you in order to create the stress of a smoke-filled environment. The last training exercise was a drill inside a tight enclosure that simulated an attempted rescue of a firefighter after a collapse. The exercise began with our breaching a wall and crawling under and around several obstacles until we came to a pipe that we had to wriggle through. It was an uncomfortable and challenging environment, and two of the four members of my team had to exit the exercise before finishing. At one point I became stuck inside the pipe, and I started to panic. I stopped and thought about it for a minute, and I told myself that if I couldn't get through the obstacle for some reason, there were people right outside who could see what I could not and would help me.

As I thought about the psalmist and the anxieties of life, it felt like that training exercise. There is so much we go through with only partial sight. We cannot see the big picture or the future. It feels like things are closing in around us and we will not make it through. For the believer, the only answer is to look to the Lord and know that He is with us in the fog of life. He is our refuge when the winds of life are beating against us. He is our confidence when the wicked rage. The psalmist says, "But the Lord has been my defense, and my God the rock of my refuge." That is the testimony of a life that has not always experienced comfort. One cannot appreciate the rock of refuge when the weather is good and the winds are tempered. However, when the storm is raging and the winds howl, there is a new appreciation for the rock that can give us refuge.

There are several things we can do that will help us with the anxieties of this life that come from past hurts and pains. First, we can think honestly about our pain. We have been hurt, and we are afraid of being hurt like that again. We have unanswered questions, and we do not know why God did not act to resolve the situation in a different manner.

Second, we can take those honest thoughts and anxieties and pour them out before the Lord. We can be honest with ourselves and with God. He already knows our needs, our questions and our anxieties, but as we pour our hearts out before God, it causes us to seek His face and recognize His character.

Third, we can trust the promises in God's Word that tell us about His character. We can know that He has greater vision, greater wisdom, and greater power than us, and He will work for His glory.

Fourth, we can recognize that God is working, and we can go forward seeking His glory even in our suffering. That is exactly what Paul did in his imprisonment and sufferings. He realized that the Lord could have delivered him out of many hardships, but by allowing him to go through suffering, the gospel was advanced, and the Lord was glorified. This perspective caused Paul to declare this to the church at Philippi: "But what things were gain to me, these I have counted loss for Christ. Yet indeed I also count all things loss for the excellence of the knowledge of Christ Jesus my Lord, for whom I have suffered the loss of all things, and count them as rubbish, that I may gain Christ and be found in Him, not having my own righteousness, which is from the law, but that which is through faith in Christ, the righteousness which is from God by faith; that I may know Him and the power of His resurrection, and the fellowship of His sufferings, being conformed to His death" (Philippians 3:7-10).

Did Paul have anxieties and pain? Yes, but he was able to move forward knowing that whatever he experienced, even through his sufferings, God was able to work for good and for His glory.

This thought returns me to those lessons from the life of Joseph that were so powerful in my own life after the train accident. It took years for Joseph to see the good that God could bring about in his life. He had been abused, enslaved, slandered and imprisoned, but in all of those things, there was one huge factor that made the difference in his life: He had faith in the Lord's power and sovereignty, and he knew that God was not going to neglect His promises. He could not be conquered, because his spirit could not be shaken. He could say in the end, "But God," because he endured the trials of his life long enough to say, as the psalmist, "But the Lord has been my defense and the rock of my refuge."

This is my prayer for you in whatever circumstance or anxiety you face in your life.

Section 2
Tabitha

God's Love

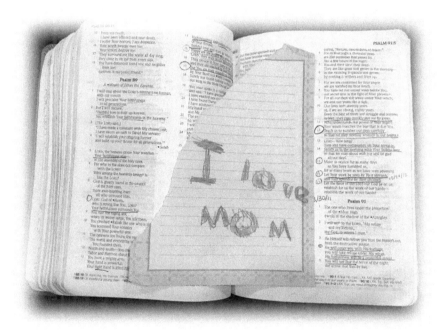

Good?

You are good, and You do what is good; teach me your statutes.
(Psalm 119:68)

What do you do after the unthinkable has happened, when you're in an "I hope this is a nightmare" place — when you are frozen, breathless, reeling and confused from something that pummels you unexpectedly? Or maybe you saw it coming but had no possible recourse. What can you do when you are utterly helpless to "fix" your situation, when there are no words to adequately describe your pain and despair? Where can you turn when your mind is spinning dizzily trying to wrap itself around the circumstances in which you find yourself?

This is where I found myself after the sudden death of our delightful, loud and beautiful six-year-old son, Benji.

One Saturday morning, all seemed right in the world. The weather was warming up, and the next day would be the first day of spring. I had a loving, supportive husband, three lively and entertaining boys, and I was almost seven and a half months into a smooth pregnancy with a little girl for whom I had prayed for years. I was busily preparing our family for an outing with the children from our church.

A few mornings later, I was prone to uncontrollable sobbing, sitting over the heat vent in our dining room with my Bible and a blanket, a billion thoughts and emotions beating around in my brain and body.

There was a palpable quietness in the house — not just the absence of noise, so much, but the acute and overwhelming awareness that something of vital importance was missing.

As I began to read passages in Psalms and Isaiah, this was the first verse that I remember really resonating with my spirit: "You are good, and You do what is good; teach me your statutes." Now, I was blessed with godly parents who instilled in me from an early age three important doctrines, among many others — one: God is good; two: God loves us unconditionally and wants the best for us; and three: God is sovereign (or, in control) even when we do not understand. I honestly do not ever remember doubting God's goodness, even in the darkest days of grief, because it had been so engrained and observed during my younger years.

(I want to pause here and say that it's okay if you do not have this same experience and assurance immediately or constantly when you are going through heartache and disaster. There are other areas where I tend to struggle, doubt and falter. This also seems to be the appropriate place for another disclaimer in case you, like myself at times, tend to read or listen to Christian writers and speakers and imagine they have magical Christian superpowers and have every aspect of their life together. I do not have it all together! For those who know me well, this is not even necessary to mention. My closet is a wreck. I cannot seem to get or stay organized. I sometimes struggle with motivation and am usually running late. We are all coming from different places and are in different stages of our Christian journey. I believe the Father can handle our questions and doubts. Our irresolution and uncertainty have no effect on God's unchanging character. His goodness and sovereignty are absolute! He will lead us gently and graciously by His Spirit to a better understanding of His character if we allow Him and look to Him and His Word.)

We had already been experiencing God's undeniable goodness over and over, like tiny sparks of light in the darkness, during the few days that had passed since the train wreck, and we would continue to experience it in other countless ways in the days and years to follow.

So my spirit was in complete agreement with the first part of the verse — the "You are good" part. It was the second part of the verse that grabbed my attention and made me feel a tiny bit uneasy and intrigued: "And you do what is good." Nothing about this situation felt good. I hesitate to even try to describe what it's like to bury a child, because I do not possess the words or ability to do so. I am not really sure adequate words even exist for such a description. Nothing about this situation looked good or sounded good. Eight years later, there are memories of certain sights and sounds that still bring me immediately to tears when I think about them.

Having grown up in a Bible-believing church and being married to a pastor, I had heard my share of sermons on Romans 8:28. I knew "all things work together for the good of those who love God: those who are called according to His purpose." I knew those words meant that not everything that happens in a world contaminated by sin and its consequences is good, but that God, in His vast knowledge and power, has a miraculous way of bringing good from difficult circumstances, pain and suffering in the lives of those who are followers of Christ in a fallen world.

I trusted that He would "someday" do that in this situation, as well. But was God "doing good" on Saturday, March 19, 2011, when a speeding kiddie train filled with unsuspecting children and adults derailed and drastically changed our lives and the lives of so many others?

Yes. There it was on the page, in black and white. He was doing good that day. God was not napping or on vacation. He wasn't distracted by something happening in China. He wasn't busy tending to more important people or larger problems. He was completely aware of every detail of what was happening in the park and the hospitals. As God of the universe, He could have tweaked thousands of tiny details and decisions that would have ultimately changed the outcome of that day. But for reasons not privy to me, He allowed the events of that day to unfold exactly as they had, and this verse was just the reassurance I needed.

Of course, the two statements "You are good" and "You do good" went together. It's like the flip side of a coin. If God was good, He had to be doing good. God's goodness and His actions could not be separated. God had a plan and purpose for our lives that I needed to trust. I needed to do what the last part of the verse says and stay in His Word so He could "teach me His statutes."

Just a few weeks later, on May 3, 2011, I marked and dated Psalm 33:4 in my Bible: "For the word of the Lord is right, and all His work is trustworthy." Trustworthy, according to Merriam-Webster, means being worthy of confidence, able to be relied upon as honest or truthful. God's goodness, His character and His Word, the Bible, can be trusted. This is where we can go when we are living a nightmare, depressed, discouraged, despondent or suffering. He longs for us to put our focus on Him during times of turmoil. He is faithful and good and capable of bringing good from any circumstance.

— In what difficult or heartbreaking situation do you find yourself today?

— Will you trust God's character and goodness?

— Will you look for and record ways He is doing good, even during bad times?

— Will you accept that He is in control and has a plan?

— Will you acknowledge that, as a believer, He is working for good in your life to bring "beauty from ashes"(Isaiah 61:3)?

— Will you commit to stay in His Word to be taught His statutes and receive the strength and comfort you need?

CARRIED TO COMPLETION

For I am sure of this, that He who started a good work in you will carry it on to completion until the day of Christ Jesus. (Philippians 1:6)

In those early days after Benji's death, it was so terribly heartbreaking to think about the future — and the present and the past, for that matter.

But the future, laden with questions, had an especially bitter sting. How would we ever have another family picture made? How could we go back to the campground at the beach where we had gone since Benji was a baby?

What if the grief was so encompassing that I messed up my children? What if I couldn't cope and ended up a slave to some awful addiction? Sometimes, when I would think about myself in the future, I would envision myself like I remembered Carol Burnett in an old television skit: long gray robe and messy hair, holding a bottle and slurring her words. It seemed so frightening to gaze out into the future.

Thankfully, the Lord began speaking to my spirit about trusting Him one minute at a time. He used words from my faith-filled mom about how what I was going through was big and that I couldn't handle it on my own. He used words from a friend about making it through one small task and then the next. He began to teach me early on about not getting too far out into the future in my mind.

Then I encountered this verse, and the Lord began to inscribe it on my heart: "He who started a good work in you will carry it on to completion." Another version says, "He will be faithful to complete it."

He had started a good work in me when I gave my life to Christ as a teenager. He had certainly been faithful. He had been so good to us during those difficult days just after the accident, showing His love and faithfulness to us in hundreds of sweet little ways. We'd had the prayers and support of a family, a church, a community and beyond. He had given us comfort and strength to make it through unimaginable and heart-wrenching circumstances.

When I thought about the words of this verse, it took some pressure off me. I knew the Lord was working through this horrible situation. We had been blessed enough to see it, feel it and hear about it. I could trust that He would continue to work, because He finishes what He starts! It wasn't all up to me to keep it together, to somehow move forward, to not mess up my kids. The Holy Spirit would continue to work in my life and circumstances.

I have looked back to that verse and drawn strength and encouragement many times in the years since Benji's death. A few years ago, when we were building our house, we decided we wanted to write Scriptures on the walls before they were painted as a fun activity and a way to acknowledge the importance of God's Word in our home. It was such a blessing to see the boys writing the verses, and to see little five-year-old Hannah draw a picture of her three brothers and herself on the wall of Seth and Matthew's room. It's comforting to know that beneath the blues and grays on those walls are verses about safety, peace, prayer, rest, serving God and the blessing of children. There's even a silly verse in the bathroom.

Beside the window of the master bedroom, underneath a peaceful shade of "Pensive Blue," this verse, Philippians 6:1, is inscribed. Some days when I'm sad or discouraged, I'll go rest my head on that wall and think about these words, and I'll remember that I can trust a faithful God to complete what He starts.

ONE WORD

Therefore, submit to God. But resist the devil and he will flee from you. (James 4:7)

Some time back, I asked a friend, "What do you think is the one single word that probably helped me most after Benji died?"

It was definitely a broad and thought-provoking question to just throw out at someone. After contemplation, the response I received was, "Heaven," which was a beautiful and appropriate answer. It does comfort me greatly to know that because of Benji's faith in Christ's death and resurrection, he is in heaven.

It also delights me to read and think about Revelation 21:4, which promises, "He will wipe away every tear from their eyes. Death will no longer exist; grief, crying and pain will exist no longer, because the previous things have passed away." For believers, these are all wonderful promises concerning heaven that we can look forward to, as well as the expectation of being reunited with other followers of Christ who have passed on before us.

I think if someone had asked me a similar question, I would have possibly answered, "Grace" or "Faithfulness," because, indeed, as the Scriptures declare, "My [God's] grace is sufficient for you, for power is perfected in weakness" (2 Corinthians 12:9a), and "Because of the Lord's faithful love we do not perish, for His mercies are new every morning; great is Your faithfulness" (Lamentations 3:22-23)!

I was well acquainted with my own weakness and can certainly attest to God's sufficient grace and faithfulness during those days of extreme grief and brokenness. However, I think the single word that probably most helped guide me to the correct perspective, posture and attitude was the word "submit."

Submit. It's not a word we use very often or even like! Honestly, it can kind of give us the "nails on a chalkboard" feeling when we hear or see it. Just the mention of the word conjures up thoughts of not getting what we want and having to bow to someone else's decisions, ideas or desires. In a world where we are taught from the earliest age to "believe in ourselves," "follow our hearts" and "look out for number one," coupled with our natural bent for wanting our own way, submission doesn't sound pleasant or inviting.

While Dwight was in seminary in North Carolina, our pastor became a dear friend and kept in touch with us through the years. Sadly, he and his wife suffered the sudden and unexpected death of their adult son a few years before Benji's death. I remember Dwight telling me not long after the train accident that he had spoken again with "Mr. Bill," as Benji called him, and he had told Dwight in the conversation to submit to the Lord's will.

This "submit" word was not even spoken directly to me, but it spoke directly to my heart! Often times, I think we understand things with our minds, but don't take them to heart and apply them. However, this time, I didn't exactly understand the word with my brain. Submit? Did I have a choice about what had happened? Could I change it? Did I have to give my permission or allow my son to die? Of course not! I rolled these thoughts and questions around inside my head, but my resonating heart knew exactly what the word meant. I had to accept God's decision not to change the heartbreaking events of March 19, 2011 — to fully trust that

He knows and does what is best, and rely on His sovereignty (supreme power and authority).

When we have the proper perspective, we realize that we are not the boss. We often spend so much time trying to control even the most minute details of our lives — and sometimes even the lives of others. When something uncontrollable and unforeseen sweeps through, we are reminded of how very little we actually control. This should not cause the believer to live in fear. Rather, it should cause us to focus on the fact that the One who has all knowledge, all wisdom, all power, who sees the beginning and the end at the same time and can bring glory to Himself and good to us, is actively and eternally in control!

You would not naturally think that submission would bring peace and freedom, but that is exactly what happened. Although my world was upside down, I had a certain peace about God's plan for Benji and for our family. I truly believe that submitting to God's purpose early helped me avoid adding layers of bitterness, guilt and anger that sometimes invade and take root in a heart that is already crushed with grief. Submitting to, and acknowledging, God's authority and control freed me from focusing on the train driver, the legal mess, what "should" have happened, what I could have done, and more. It allowed me space to grieve and to begin healing. Submission allowed me to focus on the only One who deserves total control and who has the perfect ability to execute His plan for His glory and our good.

Will you submit to God's will for your life, trusting His power, love and goodness?

— In what situations are you currently in need of peace?

— What do you need freedom from today?

— Over what difficult circumstance do you have no control?

— How can you submit to God's authority and plan in this circumstance?

Pray for the Holy Spirit to give you power to relinquish control of your life, plans, dreams and circumstances, and focus on the sovereignty of God.

Covered

*For You formed my inward parts; You covered me in my mother's
womb. (Psalm 139:13)*

During my pregnancies, the Lord led me to special Bible verses for
each of my children. These were verses that I felt somehow applied,
or would apply, to their lives, passages that the Lord used to communicate
a special truth or encouragement to me while I was carrying them.

While pregnant with Hannah, I had a calendar in our bedroom that
someone had given me displaying cute animal pictures and verses of
Scripture. I would often look at this one particular verse and be comforted
throughout the time I was carrying Hannah: "But the Lord is faithful; He
will strengthen and protect you from the evil one" (2 Thessalonians 3:3).

Although my pregnancy with Hannah was going wonderfully and I
felt great for the most part, I did not quite have the same sense of peace
and well-being that I had experienced during my pregnancies with the
boys. Maybe it was due to insecurities about my "advanced maternal
age," as the doctor at our one required visit to the maternal fetal office
repeatedly stated.

We had taken the boys with us on the day of the visit to find out if we
were having a boy or girl and to have the precautionary measurements.
They were so excited to see their sister on the screen, with blue, red and
green colors swirling around her. In typical little-boy fashion, they were
making comments about how she looked like a ninja or dragon-slayer as

the images moved about on the screen.

I don't think I will ever forget Benji's words when the doctor finally left the consultation office — after an hour or so of going over statistics, scenarios and information. He looked up from his spot on the floor (where he had resorted to rolling around) and said, "Why wouldn't that doctor ever quit talking?" That, followed by Dwight's question, "Do you feel old now?" provided us with immediate laughter and smiles for years to come.

During those months while I was pregnant with Hannah, I would glance over to the calendar in our bedroom and read the Bible verse and be comforted and reminded to trust God for strength and protection.

I also had a delivery-day tradition at each of the boys' births. While in the hospital, progressing toward delivery, I would read Psalm 139. This passage so richly and beautifully describes how the Father created us and knows us intimately, how He sees us and leads us and is always with us. Those were valuable truths worth remembering on delivery day, and would grow to become even more meaningful on the day of Hannah's arrival.

I do not have words to adequately describe the myriad thoughts and emotions we were experiencing as we waited for Hannah's arrival, just five and a half weeks after Benji's death. By nature, my personality is mostly even-keeled, and it's normally not too difficult for me to control my visible emotions. But that was not really possible for a long time after Benji's death. I would burst into tears, sometimes in front of friends or random strangers, when asked a question about my children or about Benji. People would usually end up looking at me with confusion, or with pity, or both. I would feel bad that I made them feel bad. It was quite the sad cycle of awkwardness.

Our older boys both had two broken wrists from the train accident and were dealing with the sudden loss of a little brother. I constantly had thoughts of sweet Benji in my mind — what had been, what could have been, and what never would be. I was terrified that I would forget things about him, things he had said and done, experiences we'd had, little things about him like the feel of his hair or the sound of his voice. I was in anguish over thoughts of Hannah never knowing the brother who had so sweetly named her.

While I do not have adequate words to describe the deep grief of losing a child, I have often begun to try to describe it using the words "consuming" and "encompassing" grief. It was mentally, emotionally and even physically draining during those days, and for a long time. The church was a beautiful display of the body of Christ during this time, organizing meals and cleaning for us all the way up to the time of Hannah's arrival. There was such an unbelievable outpouring of love and support from our family, friends, doctors, nurses, community and state, and even beyond. To this day, we sometimes meet people who tell us (when they find out we are Benji's family) how they have prayed for us. Without a doubt, the kindness shown to us, and especially the prayers lifted for us, helped sustain us during our darkest days.

There was a time during the day of Hannah's arrival when I found myself alone in the hospital room. Not having brought my own Bible with me, I decided to use Dwight's to read Psalm 139. The version of the Bible he had with him that day was the New King James Version. Normally, when I get to verse 13 of Psalm 139 in my Bible, I read, with beautiful familiarity, "You knit me together in my mother's womb." But on this day when I came to verse 13, it said, "You covered me in my mother's womb." Covered me. The words surged off the page and embraced my shattered heart. That was exactly what God had done for Hannah on the day of the train wreck!

My mind went back to that dreadful day in the park. On the third time around the track, the kiddie train had gained so much speed, I thought, "How are we going to make it around this curve?" Then, I could see and feel us leaving the track.

The next thing I remembered was waking up in the rocky creek, looking for Matthew, who had been seated with me, my right leg and head weak and aching, and looking over to see him sitting at the edge of the creek with blood streaming down both of his cheeks, but okay.

The sights and sounds were terrifying as I walked out of the creek and up the hill to sit for a moment. I tried to scan the area and locate my other children from my side of the bank. I spotted Seth and several of the other church kids on the grass on the opposite bank, scared and injured, but conscious. Matthew and I headed across to check on them as I kept looking for Benji. I spotted Dwight first — bleeding, hurt and stunned — and then Benji, a little farther up, lying motionless on the ground. He had been carried up from the rocks by some bystanders.

People were gathering around, working on him. I went to my son, told him it was okay, and that his mommy was there. How I hoped it would be like the movies and I would see some miraculous response to the CPR they had begun. But as I watched, I knew it was bad. I stepped away and borrowed a phone to call my mom and dad to have people start praying for Benji. By God's grace, I thought to go back and tell Seth and Matthew I was going to the hospital with Benji and then returned and followed the stretcher across the tracks, up the steps and to the ambulance. Later, the boys told us they had not seen Benji, even though he was probably lying about 125 feet from them.

I sat in the front of the ambulance, scared and quiet, as the medics worked on Benji in the back before transporting him to the ER, which was only about a mile from the park. My mind darted back to the long-awaited baby girl I was carrying, who was just jolted with me from the fast-moving kiddie train into the rocky creek. I mustered a desperate, fragmented prayer: "I would love to know this baby is okay." Almost immediately, I felt the little nudge of a tiny elbow or fist in my lower left abdomen. In fact, Hannah was positioned differently than all three of my boys had been at this point of pregnancy. They had all curled up on my right side, just under my ribs, but Hannah was nestled under the left side of my rib cage. I had landed hard on my right side. This tiny nudge was comforting to me and would help give me a sense of peace a little later after arriving at the hospital and having to choose between staying near Benji or going upstairs to have Hannah checked immediately. These were just two of the many ways God showed us His goodness on that disastrous day.

Sometime later — although I really don't know how long, as time has a weird way of morphing and distorting during events like these — my dad and I were led from a waiting/consultation room. With divine timing, we were met in the hallway by my parents' pastor and my best friend's parents. We were all led somberly to an ER room where Dwight was being treated to hear the devastating news that no parent ever wants to hear.

When the doctor and nurses later checked and monitored Hannah, they found that I was having contractions. In quiet anguish, I begged God to allow me not to deliver Hannah yet. I could not imagine planning and having our baby boy's funeral just after delivering a new baby. I always had breastfeeding difficulties in the beginning weeks after giving birth. Hannah would be about seven weeks early if they didn't get the contractions stopped. Our world was shattered and upside down. I needed time. Thankfully, my body responded to the medication, and the contractions stopped.

So, as I lay in my hospital bed the following month, preparing to give birth to Hannah, I was keenly aware of how the Lord had "covered" her in my womb. He had miraculously protected her the day the train derailed and kept her tucked away, safe and sound, until just the right time.

She had hundreds of people praying for her. Now I often tell my smart, little, zesty blonde with Benji's blue eyes about how I prayed for a little girl for a such long time and that the Lord picked out the sweetest one and gave her to me. I also tell her about all the prayers that went up for her and quip that the Lord just kept adding extra sugar and spice when creating her!

As you read the words of Psalm 139:1-18, bask in the knowledge that you, too, were created by and are seen by a loving, powerful, sovereign God who is in control, even when your circumstances are devastating, your heart is broken and you do not understand. Notice and highlight the ways He is actively caring for you when you may not see or feel Him. Ask Him for strength and protection, and trust Him to provide all that you need to make it through each minute.

¹ Lord, You have searched me and known me. ² You know when I sit down and when I stand up; You understand my thoughts from far away. ³ You observe my travels and my rest; You are aware of all my ways. ⁴ Before a word is on my tongue, You know all about it, Lord. ⁵ You have encircled me; You have placed Your hand on me. ⁶ This extraordinary knowledge is beyond me. It is lofty; I am unable to reach it. ⁷ Where can I go to escape your Spirit? Where can I flee from your presence? ⁸ If I go up to heaven, You are there; If I make my bed in Sheol, You are there. ⁹ If I live at the eastern horizon or settle at the western limits, ¹⁰ Even there Your hand will lead me; Your right hand will hold on to me. ¹¹ If I say, "Surely the darkness will hide me, and the light around me will be night"— ¹² Even the darkness is not dark to You. The night shines like the day; darkness and light are alike to you. ¹³ For it was You who created my inward parts; You knit me together [and covered (NKJV)] in my mother's womb. ¹⁴ I will praise You because I have been remarkably and wonderfully made. Your works are wonderful and I know this very well. ¹⁵ My bones were not hidden from You when I was formed in the depths of the earth. ¹⁶ Your eyes saw me when I was formless; all my days were written in your book and planned before a single one of them began. ¹⁷ God, how difficult Your thoughts are for me to comprehend; how vast their sum is! ¹⁸ If I counted them they would outnumber the grains of sand; when I wake up, I am still with You.

RIGHT-HAND MAN

Do not fear, for I am with you: do not be afraid, for I am your God.
I will strengthen you; I will help you; I will hold onto you with my
righteous right hand. (Isaiah 41:10)

The verse above from Isaiah has long been one of my favorites, and after the train accident, it seemed to be popping up everywhere — in devotional readings, in my personal Bible study, and in sympathy card after sympathy card.

I suppose God so often commands us in Scripture not to fear because our human hearts tend to be so prone to fear instead of faith. Quite honestly, there is a lot to fear in our broken world if we are not constantly looking through eyes of faith!

One of my earliest childhood memories is being in the emergency room as a two-year-old little girl, awaiting stitches after toppling backwards off the picnic table and cutting my head on a toy truck. As I lay there restrained, scared and crying, I remember my sweet mama reciting Psalm 56:3 to me: "What time I am afraid, I will trust in Thee."

Then, thirty-seven years later, I had stood in the emergency room of the same hospital and been given life-shattering news about my beautiful, precious six-year-old son sustaining injuries too severe to survive. I had prayed earlier in the waiting room, acknowledging and believing that God could heal his broken little body, knowing nothing is too hard for an all-powerful God. He chose to answer my prayer differently than I had hoped. I lowered my head to my sobbing husband's chest and whispered through tears, "We will get through this together, with the Lord's help."

Experiencing something so traumatic and devastating has a way of putting things in perspective and reminding us that we are not in control. I was weak, tired and small, and the temptation was to focus on the unknown, the future, the dangers and all the horrible things that could possibly happen. But this is not what the Lord wants for us. He says with authority, "Do not fear!" "I am with you." "Do not be afraid." "I am your God." "I will strengthen you." And, "I will help you." I was aware that if I was going to make it through something so crushing and overwhelming, it was going to only be with His help and strength. I needed to hear the reassurances from the first parts of this verse over and over again, and the Lord was providing that.

As a special bonus, the last part of this verse, "I will hold onto you with my righteous right hand," was like a personal little God-wink.

When I was pregnant with Benji, we had narrowed down the name search to Benjamin, meaning "son of my right hand," and Gabriel, meaning "messenger." Seth still had his opinion in the mix, wanting to call the third little Easler boy Samuel, which means "God has heard." The baby's due date was December 7, 2004. Dwight suggested that if the baby was born in November, we should name him Benjamin. However, should he come in December, we would call him Gabriel, because Gabriel was the angel sent to announce the birth of Jesus.

I went into labor on November 23. At the hospital, my sister-in-law suggested that we take Seth's name choice and make Benji's middle name "Samuel." So, Benjamin Samuel Easler was born on November 24, 2004, the day before Thanksgiving. That Christmas season, Benji loved sitting in his bouncy seat in front of the Christmas tree and gazing at the lights. I remember how little five-year-old Seth would sit and hold him and how he told us on several occasions, referring to his new baby brother, "This is the best Christmas present ever!" Many times since Benji's death, I have thought with gratitude about the fact that he came thirteen days before his due date and have thanked God for allowing us a little "extra" time with him.

On one occasion when Benji was probably five or so, the youth minister was delivering the children's sermon one Sunday. During the introduction, he asked if any of the kids knew what their names meant. He proceeded to tell what a couple of names meant, then he said, "And Benji means hurricane." The congregation erupted in laughter as Benji grinned from ear to ear. No doubt, Benji was lively, loud and boisterous, but with a sweet and cuddly side. He could leave a trail of spaghetti-sauce fingerprints and toys, but also a trail of echoing laughter and his own special "Benji yell" (that he made by rolling his Rs) reverberating in his wake.

The youth pastor then went on to explain that the name Benjamin really meant "son of my right hand," or "right-hand man." The connotation is someone who is right there with you, someone on whom you can depend. Benji truly always enjoyed being right there with me. He even had a "mama song" he would lovingly sing when he was little. I will always cherish the memory, and the picture, of him right there with his daddy putting together Hannah's crib, helping us get ready for her arrival, being our little right-hand man.

A quick search of the English Standard Version of the Bible on the Accordance app shows that the words "right hand" are found in Scripture 141 times. The words often signify strength, authority, direction or favor. What a beautiful promise to sum up this verse: "I will hold onto you with my righteous right hand." Our just and good Father, who always does what is right, is holding on to us with his strong, all-powerful hand.

How I needed His hand to hold up my frail and weakened being. Each time I read the words "right hand" at the end of the verse, I felt a special connection to this truth, as if God were reminding me that this verse was especially for me and my situation. I also trusted that God was holding on to our little "right-hand man" that day in the park and now, in His presence.

What a comfort it is to know that as believers in Christ we do not have to fear. The almighty creator of the universe is always with us, ready to help and strengthen us, holding us steadily in the grip of His powerful hand.

— What fears are weighing heavily on you today?

— In the space below, thank God for His promise to strengthen, help and hold onto you during these difficult times. Ask Him to help you focus on Him in faith rather than your fears.

— Read slowly over the words of these verses and this old hymn, and return to them over and over in your mind today:

But now, thus says the Lord, who created you, O Jacob, And He who formed you, O Israel: "Fear not, for I have redeemed you; I have called you by your name; You are Mine. When you pass through the waters, I will be with you; And through the rivers, they shall not overflow you. When you walk through the fire, you shall not be burned, Nor shall the flame scorch you. (Isaiah 43:1-2)

"How Firm a Foundation" (verses 2, 3 and 4):

> *Fear not, I am with thee, O be not dismayed,*
> *For I am thy God, and will still give thee aid;*
> *I'll strengthen thee, help thee, and cause thee to stand,*
> *Upheld by My righteous, omnipotent hand.*
>
> *When through the deep waters I call thee to go,*
> *The rivers of sorrow shall not overflow;*
> *For I will be with thee, thy troubles to bless,*
> *And sanctify to thee thy deepest distress.*
>
> *When through fiery trials thy pathway shall lie,*
> *My grace, all sufficient, shall be thy supply;*
> *The flame shall not hurt thee; I only design*
> *Thy dross to consume, and thy gold to refine.*

FAITHFUL

He will cover you with His feathers; you will take refuge under His wings. His faithfulness will be a protective shield. (Psalm 91:4)

As I reread the verse above, my mind is flooded with images. When I think about feathers, faithfulness, refuge, wings and shields, I am overcome with sweet memories of Benji and his brothers, and of God's goodness.

I remember the day of the "big boys'" last Upward basketball game in February 2011. The coach of Matthew's team, the Eagles, had generously asked if Benji would like to run onto the court with his brother's team. As loud music began to pump into the gym, out ran Benji, leading the team, arms flapping, circling the gym with delight like the team's own little Eagle mascot.

I also think about our 2008 Vacation Bible School and how the kids had sung the song "Untitled Hymn," with all the verses and motions, over and over that year. Some months later, Dwight was asked to do the devotional message at a local nursing home. I thought it would be nice for the boys, who were about nine, seven and four, to join me in singing the song and doing the motions for the residents. The boys were completely over the song at that point, and they not so enthusiastically flapped their arms as the end of the song echoed, "And with your final heartbeat, kiss the world goodbye. Then go in peace and laugh on glory's side, and fly to Jesus. Fly to Jesus ... fly to Jesus ... and live." I will always remember a wise and frail little lady who caught my arm as we were leaving and said, "You've got a gold mine with all these boys — a gold mine!"

I smile as I remember capes and costumes, swords and shields, and the sound of plastic weapons clacking and buzzing during light saber battles. But one of my most vivid "wing" memories involves Benji standing on the pew beside me at the last church service he would ever attend. On Sunday evening, March 13, Benji and I sat at the back right side of the church. As the congregation sang "I'll Fly Away," Benji began to flap his arms and sing. I got his attention and gave him a smile with enough of a grimace to say, "Let's not get carried away." He continued to flap and sing as I stood there singing, feeling amused and a little self-conscious and having no idea just how soon he would be "flying away."

On March 30, my eleventh morning without my baby boy, I sat down over the dining room heat vent to read my Bible and try to find strength and comfort to make it through another day. During that time I remember feeling that every morning was like a fresh punch in the gut. Every morning, the painful reality that Benji was gone set in again.

But there was something else that I found to be new every morning: God's faithfulness. According to Lamentations 3:22-24, "Because of the Lord's faithful love we do not perish, for His mercies never end. They are new every morning; great is your faithfulness! I say: The Lord is my portion, therefore I put my hope in Him."

I had been finding help and comfort in Psalms and Isaiah, and as I opened my Bible to read from Psalms that morning, I discovered a jagged piece of blue paper that had been torn from my notes journal one Sunday night the previous December. The words "I love MOM" were written in bubble letters and scribbled in with pencil. It was tucked between the pages that included Psalm 88:15 through 91:5. Through a fresh river of tears, I began to read the treasures packed in these pages, and specifically Psalm 91.

On the top left side of my Bible, Psalm 89 begins, "I will sing about the Lord's faithful love forever; with my mouth I will proclaim your faithfulness to all generations." The rest of the chapter continues to describe God's power, magnificent strength and faithfulness. On the bottom right side of the pages was the beginning of Psalm 91, which portrays God's protection and faithfulness.

I love how the end of Psalm 91:4 declares, "His faithfulness will be a protective shield." I've seen enough superhero movies with the kids to know that a protective shield is definitely something I am interested in having. When I hear the words "protective shield," I imagine a clear bubble, or force field, completely surrounding someone, and whatever is shot or hurled at them bounces off the impenetrable surface.

Looking back, I can say that God's faithfulness has indeed been a protective shield. As I trusted Him to get me through those first minutes, hours and days, He faithfully supplied what I needed. Then the next minute, hour or day, He graciously continued to provide the strength and comfort I needed for that moment. Day after heartbreaking day, event after event, special occasion after special occasion, He was faithfully there, sprinkling His grace through a Scripture verse, a song, a once-forgotten memory resurfacing, or an understanding word or smile. He would remind us of His faithfulness through someone's small — but not really small at all — act of kindness, such as being called out early from a full waiting room (when the train wreck coverage was still on the news, and the comment "You look familiar" was regularly heard). Every day, God showed us His faithfulness in many ways.

Psalm 91 also has much to say about God's protection. We had an abundance of rain the spring that Benji died. This was strangely comforting to me. I felt like nature was rightfully weeping with me. I imagined Creation crying along in acknowledgement that such a delightful child no longer romped about the earth.

Not only was there an abundance of rain that spring, there was also an abundance of storms. One of our boys had not liked storms since he was a toddler, and this fear was extremely heightened after the train accident and Benji's death. When storms came, he insisted that the family go to the basement or hallway. I wrote several Bible verses on a sheet of notebook paper, including most of Psalm 91. When storms came, we sat together and read those verses. I have a pretty vivid memory of lying in the hallway with the family, me with my very pregnant belly, trying to get comfortable with pillows around me. Thankfully, those fears later subsided, but occasionally I run across that piece of notebook paper tucked away somewhere, and it serves as a reminder of God's faithfulness and protection during such a painful time.

And then there were the rainbows! Yes, we had a tremendous amount of rain and plentiful storms, but we also had an unusual number of rainbows for quite a while. As you know, we found Benji's last little kindergarten drawing, a rainbow, in his book bag a few days after the accident. Afterward, with every rainbow that came, there was a sense that God knew exactly what we were experiencing, that He saw and had a plan and would remain faithful.

I notated some of the rainbow sightings and dates in a helpful devotional book I was going through at the time. There was a rainbow after the kid's Easter musical, when I was missing seeing Benji up there singing; a rainbow when I was taking the GA girls to class on a day I had felt so sad; a rainbow at VBS; and a rainbow after Hannah's baby dedication. Someone sent me a picture of a rainbow in Spartanburg on the afternoon that Benji died. On an afternoon that school started back, I was there, walking and letting little Hannah play, and I spotted a rainbow over the church and graveyard. Someone also sent me a beautiful picture of a rainbow over the park the weekend it reopened. It seemed like there were rainbows and double rainbows popping up everywhere at opportune times. Maybe there had always been that many rainbows and I had not noticed, but I do not think so. I believe it was God working, in His sovereignty, to show us a visible reminder of His love, provision and faithfulness.

I love how Psalm 42:8 says, "The Lord will send His faithful love by day; His song will be with me in the night," and how Psalm 94:18-19 states, "If I say, 'My foot is slipping,' your faithful love will support me, Lord. When I am filled with cares, your comfort brings me joy."

May I encourage you with the truth of God's faithfulness? It's part of His perfect and divine character. He is always faithful. When I have not been faithful, when I've been distracted or put things or people ahead of Him or tried to find satisfaction in something other than Him, He has always remained forgiving and faithful. It's who He is. Will you trust His faithfulness to cover your mind and heart like a protective shield? Will you rest in the beauty that His faithfulness is new every morning?

THINGS THAT HELPED ME: TIPS FOR GRIEVING

Stay in God's Word

This is probably the single most important piece of advice I can offer someone who has suffered a great loss or is going through something devastating. As believers in Christ, we have the promise that the Holy Spirit is our Comforter. He will comfort us in many ways, but primarily through His Word, the Bible. After Benji's death, some days this was the only comfort I found. Looking back on those days of extreme pain and heartbreak, I have many sweet memories of how God held and strengthened me as I came to Him in total dependence. By focusing on His character, His promises, and the eternal truths of His Word, God provided the sustaining hope and grace I needed.

Listen to Christian music

I could not even begin to list all the ways the Lord has used music to seep into the cracks of my broken heart and administer soothing, calming relief to my soul and bind up my aching heart. So often the perfect song, at just the right time, has brought me help and encouragement.

I remember this happening the first time I drove back by the park a few weeks after the train wreck, or while in church, on special occasions, and on multiple first days of school. For a long time, "back to school" and the days leading up were just as rough on me as any holiday, and probably the worst time of the year other than the anniversary of Benji's death. After years of tender messages through songs, I began to almost look forward to getting in the car on that first day of school and turning on the radio to see how the Lord would speak through music.

I can look back and see how, even before Benji's death, God was working to prepare my heart. In the weeks before the accident, I began to hear a new song by Kerrie Roberts called "No Matter What." The melody was upbeat and catchy, but the words always seemed to snag my heart, especially the chorus:

No matter what, I'm going to love You.
No matter what, I'm going to need You.
I know that You can find a way to keep me from the pain.
But if not, I'll trust You anyway — no matter what.

Whenever that song played, I would hear a nagging question in my spirit: "Will you?" It made me uncomfortable, and I would begin to think about scenarios and things that could possibly go wrong, or things that might be wrong with my soon-to-be-born Hannah (considering my "advanced maternal age"). I would try to push the song out of my head until the next time.

One afternoon on the highway, while I was making the thirty-five minute drive to Spartanburg for a routine OB-GYN appointment, the song began to play. The same question returned to my mind: "Will you trust me? Will you love me? No matter what?" This time I whispered aloud, "Yes."

In the days after the accident, I began to really listen to the words of the verses, with phrases about holding onto God's promises, heartache having to go through God's hands before it can touch our lives, and not possibly being able to make it without the Lord's help, hope and strength. They, too, took on special meaning and brought me peace.

Journal

Journaling was therapeutic for me after Benji's death. Writing down my thoughts and feelings helped me sort through all the anguish I was feeling. I could write about Benji, fears, dreams and memories. I wrote down meaningful Scripture verses the Lord was using to strengthen me. I wrote prayers and pleas for help. I wrote a poem called "Grief Psalm" that vividly spoke about the myriad ways grief was always with me, but went on to say how the Lord was always there, as well. I filled two spiral notebooks with these types of sentiments.

During the writing of this book, these journals have been the source of much stress for me. I have already alluded to my organizational challenges, but I knew exactly where my journals were when we moved just down the road a few years ago. I removed them from the blue tub at some point and thought I knew where I had put them, but they still have not been located, even after much prayer and searching. I finally had to resolve that maybe there was a reason they were not to be found; maybe the rawness of those words would have encumbered me and further slowed down my writing pace (which was already turtle speed). Maybe the depth, intensity and expression of the pain I felt was not what I needed to focus on, but rather the faithfulness and goodness of our Heavenly Father who provides for our every need.

A dear lady at church also brought me a pretty journal that I used to write entries to Benji. I would write to him on special occasions and holidays about events or special dates, sharing thoughts, information and feelings. It was a way to feel like we were still connected — a small way to include him and his memory on meaningful occasions.

Try expressing your memories and thoughts through journaling. Also, keep a record of prayers and Scriptures God is using in your life.

Be thankful!

Maybe this sounds cliché. Maybe it sounds like something people suggest when trying to make you feel better or make themselves feel better or move you forward. Maybe you think the idea of being thankful is ridiculous, and you have nothing for which to be thankful in the midst of your devastation. But that is not the case. Gratitude has an amazing way of protecting our attitudes and outlook. It shows humility before our Heavenly Father, the generous giver of all good gifts.

This can be a struggle in some seasons of life, and a more difficult task for some than others, but thankfulness is a beautiful gift that can be cultivated and improved. No matter your situation, I promise: You have things for which to be thankful. Philippians 4:8 reminds us, "Whatever is true, whatever is honorable, whatever is just, whatever is pure, whatever is lovely, whatever is commendable — if there is any moral excellence and if there is any praise — dwell on these things."

Most often, our biggest battleground is in our minds. Hurt, bitterness and anger can grow to gargantuan proportions until they clutter and control the entire mind. Satan delights to help us morph and nurse misunderstandings and pain into bondage. Train your mind to look for the lovely, pure, honorable, commendable, excellent things.

I have found it helpful during difficult times to write down a list of things for which I am grateful. Write down little things, big things — anything! Keep adding to your list.

It does not mean that you feel thankful for your circumstances or your situation. It does mean you acknowledge your past, present and future blessings, provisions, mercies, and gifts. Doing this can bring God's goodness back into focus. Cultivating this attitude can protect and free you and prepare you to heal.

Grief and gratitude can coexist.

Say no to living in guilt

Guilt has its rightful place in our lives. Feeling guilty can alert us to the need to check our relationship with God and others. It can nudge us to make things right between ourselves and those we have wronged, whether intentionally or unintentionally. It can help us be aware of a sinful act or attitude we need to confess and turn away from in repentance.

However, God does not intend for us to carry a continual burden of guilt. Colossians 2:13-14 states, "And when you were dead in trespasses and in the uncircumcision of your flesh, He made you alive with Him and forgave us all our trespasses. He erased the certificate of debt, with its obligations, that was against us and opposed to us, and has taken it out of the way by nailing it to the cross." If we have come to Christ in faith and repentance, the debt that we owed has been cancelled and forgiven through Christ's death on the cross. He took our guilt upon Himself, and we are to enjoy the freedom we receive from Him. So if we are no longer considered guilty after being forgiven of our sins, we certainly should not live in self-imposed guilt over things we cannot change. It is the Enemy's desire to bind and paralyze us and make us believe we should punish ourselves.

Often, when grieving, we think of things we should or could have done differently, things we wish we had said or not said, or ways we think we could have changed the outcome of our current situation. I believe it is normal for these thoughts to come into our minds. However, I decided early in the grieving process that I was going to try not to let guilt get a grip and linger in my mind. I knew that Benji loved his mama and would not want me to feel guilt about what had happened. The night the family went to the funeral home to view Benji's body, Matthew said, "Benji would want us to live a happy life." I truly believe Benji would want that.

It helped me to think about all the wonderful people and rich experiences Benji was blessed with in his six years. I would recall places we had been as a family and things the Lord had divinely arranged for Benji to experience. It also helped me to remember that God is ultimately in control of life and death, not me.

Focus on God's forgiveness and freedom rather than inflicting guilt and punishment on yourself.

Talk to someone

Grief is so personal, and there is so much that has to be worked through on one's own, but that does not mean we have to suffer alone. I remember the strange comfort of being around others who had experienced the death of a child. I remember how I paid close attention to the words they spoke or wrote, feeling an undesired but strong connection and appreciation. I remember thinking that if they could make it, I could.

Thankfully, Dwight was also willing to talk about what we were going through. Although we experienced the same loss, at times we were grieving differently and had different thoughts, feelings, perceptions and ways of dealing with our loss. I remember how therapeutic it was for us to go out together for some small errand. He would often just continue to drive for miles, and we would talk. We would try to sort through what had happened the day of the train wreck, comparing my memories and his, and piecing together details as if working on some sad, delicate puzzle. I remember sharing with him on numerous occasions how thankful I was that he was okay on the day of the accident and acknowledging that, in many ways, he knew what I was experiencing.

Ask God to provide the right people for you to talk with about your grief and loved one.

Rest

As I have already mentioned, deep grief is consuming and exhausting. At a time when your emotions are already all over the place, it is important to get the renewal that comes from sleep and rest.

I am a night owl. I just enjoy staying up late. After Benji's death, I would often stay up late, when everything was quiet, and look at pictures of him on the computer, savoring the little things about him that I didn't ever want to forget. I guess it was a time to think about and process everything that had happened, and how different things were. Even though I would stay up late, I normally was blessed to be able to go to sleep when I was ready. I found out later that a friend of mine was praying three specific things for me, one of which was that I could sleep and get the rest I needed.

There were, however, a handful of nights I had difficulty getting to sleep. One of those nights was when Hannah was still a newborn. During that time when I was up every few hours nursing her, I kept Christian music playing on the radio through the night. On this particular night as I lay awake, missing Benji, the song "Better Is One Day" began playing on the radio. It's taken from Psalm 84:10: "Better is one day in your courts than a thousand anywhere else. I would rather be at the door (or be a doorkeeper) of the house of my God than to live in the tents of wicked people." As the melody permeated the room, the realization hit me that Benji was dwelling in God's presence and that nothing he was missing here could compare to what he was experiencing in heaven. It calmed my mind enough to allow me to get to sleep.

Try to give your body and mind time for rest and renewal.

Get out and exercise

Okay, I will admit that the exercise part came later in my grief journey. Initially, the getting outside part often consisted of me sitting on the front porch in the swing, snuggling Hannah and crying, but there was still something helpful about getting outside. Feeling the warm sun and seeing the beauty of nature was reassuring. A little later on, after I experienced some of the positive emotional and physical effects of getting out and exercising (with just my thoughts and some good music, or sometimes with a couple of friends), I wished I had started sooner.

Resolve to get out a little each day.

Be gracious and forgiving

Let's face it. During times of devastating loss, most people don't know what to say to the person who is hurting. I am one of those people. I am always wondering, "Should I bring it up? Do they want to talk about it? What would I say?" Most likely, at the heart of some of those awkward questions is the knowledge and reality that there are really no words to fix the deep pain and grief someone is experiencing when something so precious is suddenly gone and when life seems shattered and ruined.

Although it's usually unintentional, people can sometimes say some insensitive, hurtful things. Coupled with the heightened sensitivity of the grieving person, one may leave the conversation thinking, "How could they say that to me?"

The flip side is that sometimes people act as if nothing has happened. They truly may not know what has happened, or they may not want to mention it and make you "remember" it or upset you. This can leave the grieving person thinking, "Could they not even acknowledge something completely life-shattering has just occurred?"

I found it's helpful to have a gracious attitude and assume that people are not trying to cause you further pain; they just may not know what to say or how to act around you. Remember that your Heavenly Father knows exactly what you're experiencing. He is the only One who can give true and lasting satisfaction and provide for all your needs. We must not expect or rely on others to do so. Although no one's words ever magically took away my pain, I still recall helpful words planted on the day of Benji's death and the following days — words the Lord nurtured, grew and used to help and heal.

Remember that none of us has the right words all the time. Do not dwell on hurtful or insensitive comments.

Don't be too hard on yourself

This goes hand in hand with not allowing guilt to take root in your life. Allow yourself time and space to grieve.

I needed a lot of quiet time to contemplate, cry, remember and sort through things in my mind. For a long time, it seemed like I grieved every little thing — all the things I missed about Benji, and all the things he would miss. While driving down the road after taking the boys to school, I would often realize I was holding my hand over my heart, as if trying to hold the shattered pieces together. I didn't so much as throw out an empty bottle from the refrigerator that Benji had touched without grieving one less physical connection I had to my little boy. Before that first Christmas, I found myself crawling around the living room, picking up hidden pine needles from the edges of the room. I placed them gingerly in a little porcelain box because they were from Benji's last Christmas tree. Years into my grief journey, I sat in the bathroom floor and wept after a perfume bottle that Benji had sprayed fell onto the floor and broke.

In those early days, I felt good if I had accomplished one thing during a day. For a while, you may not feel like doing much of anything. I found it was good to push myself to do a little more than I felt like, but not to put pressure on myself. It was good for me to get back to church quickly and be around people who loved and supported me, but I stepped away from my duties for a while. I had already planned not to go back to my part-time job of teaching four-year kindergarten at the church preschool after Hannah's birth so that I could stay home with her. In the weeks leading up to her birth, I did not go back to work.

Dwight, on the other hand, after a few weeks, seemed to need to feel like he was accomplishing things and improving things. He was ready to get back to work. I remember him talking about the difficulty of focusing after returning. You will have to base these types of decisions on what is best for you in your situation.

People grieve differently, and we had to be careful to communicate during that time. Dwight could tolerate longer social interactions than I could, and this would sometimes cause friction if he committed us to go to some party, social gathering or event I did not wish to attend.

Everything was suddenly very different for the entire family. We wanted the boys, when they were ready, to be able to continue to do things they enjoyed. Friends and family lavishly gave them love and gifts and spent time with them. We would go out as a family and try to do things that were fun for them and a distraction from the pain we all felt. It was a new situation for the whole family, and we had to stick together and not be too hard on ourselves or on each other.

Find practical ways to remember and celebrate your loved one

There is usually a sense of dread around the holidays or special occasions after the loss of a loved one. I remember the first time I heard a Christmas carol during that first Christmas season without Benji. I was walking through Walmart, weeks before Christmas, when I heard it playing. Pangs of joy and sadness darted through me at the same time. I had always loved Christmas time, but this season would be so different, so heartbreaking.

It was Hannah's first Christmas, and she would be old enough to enjoy it. Oh, how I wanted to keep it special for the kids! We had learned from Benji's birthday — which happened to be on Thanksgiving that first year — that special occasions, although heart-wrenching, were not always as bad as we feared they would be. The entire family gathered at my mom and dad's house, and we wrote messages to Benji on balloons and released them after we ate and celebrated my niece's birthday. It was a sweet time, and a way to show that he was not forgotten. We also learned that sometimes the day before or after the special occasion could be worse than the special occasion itself.

At Christmas time, we asked the owner of the tree farm where we always went as a family if we could cut down a tiny Christmas tree for Benji's grave. He generously gave us the little tree, free of charge. The family wrote messages on ornaments. I also purchased some ornaments that had special significance. Some people from the church added ornaments to Benji's tree. Each year, we continue to put a little tree on Benji's grave at Christmas time. Each Christmas, as a church project, we invite members to wrap their Samaritan's Purse shoeboxes in blue paper and donate them in memory of Benji around his birthday.

I could not bear to consider not hanging Benji's Christmas stocking alongside ours. We began a tradition that first Christmas of looking through the Relief magazines we received and letting the kids pick out items they wanted to donate to people in need in Benji's memory. We cut out pictures of chickens, milk, Bibles — or whatever they chose — and stuffed them into Benji's stocking.

There was another way I tried to remember Benji and connect Hannah to the brother she never met. From the time she was a baby, I would tell her that Benji loved her and that he would want me to give her kisses from him since he was not there to give them. I would give her "Benji kisses" along her face. I noted in my devotion book that at ten months old, Hannah would point to Benji's picture on the fridge and say, "Jee." She has grown up looking at pictures and hearing stories about her brother in heaven who chose her name.

Our church, friends and family raised money for new playground equipment at the church, complete with a beautiful sign with pictures of Benji on it. We had a special dedication service for the playground and have had other special services and projects to remember Benji and celebrate God's faithfulness. These are just a few practical ways we remember Benji. They seem to help take a little bit of the sting out of some of the special occasions.

Find meaningful, practical ways to remember your loved one.

Accept that you may respond and react differently than before

Daily occurrences or circumstances that you thought little of or handled easily before may leave you nervous, on edge, scared or upset. When Hannah was a baby and, later, a toddler, I remember how I responded when she received some small injury. I would become physically weak and nervous. I would usually sit down and hold her and begin to cry. I would be overcome with sadness, as my mind would go back to how Benji died. I would whisper, "I'm so sorry," as I thought of what he possibly went through that day.

Hearing an ambulance when my children were not with me would also make my insides turn to Jello until I found out what or where the incident was or that my family was okay. Even today, when a football player from either team is injured on the field, I am calm on the outside but often shaky and scared on the inside.

These are just a few examples of how reactions and responses can be affected by trauma, but there are countless ways that one may respond differently to situations and people. For me, I have found that the intensity of these feelings and reactions has lessened over time.

There was another place we had to trust the Lord with our fears and the unknown. Were we thrilled when the boys wanted to get season passes to Carowinds, the amusement park, relatively soon after they were injured and their brother was killed on a kiddie ride? Absolutely not! Were we proud of them for not living in fear because of what had happened? Absolutely! It was a true testament to God's grace and healing that they would even ask. We decided to try to work through our personal fears and allow them to get the tickets. We did not want to foster fear, bondage and defeat.

Rather than becoming a slave to fear, we must call to mind what is true. We find the truth in God's Word:

— God is in control (Colossians 1:17)
— God will never leave us or forsake us (Deuteronomy 31:8)
— He is strong when we are weak (2 Corinthians 12:10)
— Safety is of the Lord (Psalm 4:8)
— He is close to the brokenhearted (Psalm 34:18)
— He gives strength to the powerless (Isaiah 40:29)
— Our protector never slumbers or sleeps (Psalm 121:4)
— His grace is sufficient (2 Corinthians 12:9)
— He is working for our good (Romans 8:28)
— Our momentary light affliction is producing for us an absolutely incomparable weight of glory (2 Corinthians 4:17)

Yes, you may react and respond differently than before, but the Lord can help you work through these responses and feelings. There are also many good Christian counselors available if you feel you need to talk with someone about the changes, overwhelming grief and struggles you are experiencing.

Filter everything through God's love

A short time after the accident, I went to a little flip-calendar I had in the dining room and decided to look and see what was written on March 19. It was just a short little part of a verse, but it packed a powerful message: "I have loved you with an everlasting love" (Jeremiah 31:3). On March 19, the worst day of my life, I was not forgotten, overlooked or unloved. Benji was not ignored or abandoned by God. My family and sweet church friends were not deserted in the park. We were still actively being loved by the One who created us and sent His Son to die for us. My lack of understanding did not change God's everlasting love. According to Merriam-Webster's thesaurus, some synonyms for everlasting are abiding, ceaseless, endless, eternal, permanent, unending, enduring, imperishable, indestructible, timeless, stable, steady, and unfailing!

When you are broken and shattered, I pray that you will rest in the knowledge of His perfect love. I pray for you to understand that you have a purpose, even in the depths of despair. Your purpose, and mine, is to glorify God. Ask Him to guide you to do this on good days and bad. I understand how difficult it is to be in a place of complete brokenness, and I hope I have not made this journey sound easy or smooth. I hope I have pointed you to God's all-sufficient grace and never-ending mercies, which He extended to me moment by moment and day by day when I had no strength of my own. He longs to extend the same grace and mercy to you.

As I leave you with the context around the Jeremiah verse, I pray that you will find favor in the wilderness, rest, rebuilding — and, even someday, dancing — as you look minute by minute to the One who is extending His faithful love to you.

───────────────────────

This is what the Lord says: They found favor in the wilderness — all the people who survived the sword. When Israel went to find rest, the Lord appeared to him from far away. I have loved you with an everlasting love; therefore I have continued to extend faithful love to you. Again I will build you so that you will be rebuilt, Virgin Israel. You will take up your tambourines again and go out in joyful dancing. You will plant vineyards again on the mountains of Samaria; the planters will plant and will enjoy the fruit. (Jeremiah 31:2-5)

SECTION 3
MATTHEW

GOD'S PROMISE

Beginning on the next page is a contribution from our son Matthew.

The often silent grief of my boys worried me through the years. I remember asking a counselor what I needed to do to help them talk about the death of their baby brother. The counselor told me, "I think they will do better than you. It's easier for a child to trust the Lord in these times." Some of their hard times still stick deep in my soul: the stunningly painful utterances of grief by Seth as he cried out and said he should have protected Benji, and Matthew's crying in the night, wishing it was a dream.

However, now, years later, I see truly the power of God to work for good in my boys. When I see Seth as a career firefighter working with patients, I am filled with joy knowing that the Lord has given him a heart to serve others. Hearing them both talk about discipleship and evangelism and reaching their friends fills my heart with praise, knowing that the Lord has truly worked, in power.

The following section was given to me the day before the start of Matthew's senior year in high school. Words cannot express how grateful I am that you can see these words on paper. It is an opportunity to see how you can have a real relationship with Jesus Christ and also how, by faith, the power of God can sustain you in times of difficulty.

— D.E.

Truly, I say to you, unless you turn and become like children, you will never enter the kingdom of heaven. (Matthew 18:3, ESV)

Faith is often misunderstood in our world today. Faith is not merely having "religion" or "spirituality." It is not just believing that God is real. Having faith in Christ is even more than believing that Jesus lived and died and rose again.

True biblical faith certainly includes all of these things, but the essence of saving faith in Christ is a reliant trust in Him. It is not enough to merely intellectually know the truths of the gospel. Do those truths direct your heart to trust in Christ, to rely on Him and His sacrificial death and mighty resurrection? When God regenerates a sinner through the power of His Holy Spirit, He changes that person's heart, which was formerly unable to trust in Christ; He gives a new heart with new desires for God and a newfound faith in Christ — a loving communion between the regenerated sinner and the Almighty God.

Second Corinthians 5:17-18 says, "Therefore, if anyone is in Christ, he is a new creation. The old has passed away; behold, the new has come. All this is from God, who through Christ reconciled us to himself." Through this Scripture, we see that this regeneration of the heart is wrought through the mighty, supernatural work of God through Jesus Christ on the cross. Because of this work of God, we are graciously given a trusting relationship with the Father.

I have said these things to clarify my next statements, as they deal with what it means to trust God in difficult times. It must be understood first, however, that without saving faith in Christ, it is impossible to find peace and comfort in God. An unsaved person may go to great lengths to find relief from the pains and heartaches in this world, turning to vices like drugs, alcohol, or relationships. The unbeliever might even find some sort of false hope outside of Christ, turning to friendships or morality or therapy, or some false religion. It must be understood that any hope found outside of Christ is, in the end, vanity, and its result is destruction. Worldly means may ease a man's burdens temporarily, but they cannot fix the problem of the unbeliever's wicked, unrepentant, dead heart. Only Christ can heal the stains of sin before a holy God and provide a lasting joy and comfort from the griefs of this world. Unbelieving sinner, if you do not know Christ in true faith, turn to Him, and cry out for Him to save you from your sins, that you would be spared from the coming wrath, and that you may enter into His loving arms as an adopted child of God. He is willing and able to save you if you would turn to Him. Otherwise, you will find no lasting rest or safety. "'There is no peace,' says the Lord, 'for the wicked.'"

Knowing these things, we may move on to how this faith, this trusting relationship with the Father, can help us through times of suffering, grief, and doubt. I chose Matthew 18:3 as my guiding Scripture because it strongly portrays the nature of a Christian's faith. Jesus says, "Truly, I say to you, unless you turn and become like children, you will never enter the kingdom of heaven." Why is it necessary to become like a child to enter God's kingdom? Simply, because children trust what we tell them. A child does not question an adult's authority or wisdom; the child simply trusts. In the same way, we are to simply trust that what God says is true, and that He keeps His promises.

I have seen the power of childlike faith in my own life. I was saved at the age of seven, and at the time of the train wreck when my brother died, I was eight. As one might imagine, I was not very mature as a Christian at that point. However, during that very difficult time in my life, God graced me with the gift of simple faith. My grandpa tells a story, though I cannot remember this happening, of when we were at Benji's funeral and someone asked me if I would like to go see Benji one last time before they closed the casket. My response was, "Why would I go look into the casket again? He's not there. He's in heaven." I could be assured of this because, by God's sovereign grace, Benji put his faith in Christ before he passed away. His grace helped me in other areas, also, in keeping me from doubt or hatred. It must be made very clear that I was not strong in myself, but it was only God's grace that sustained me, and it was only by His grace that I had that simple faith. Still, to this day, I long for that kind of faith.

Will you simply trust in God's promises today? Yes, as Christians, we have the gift of saving faith in Christ, but it is good also to pray for greater faith, a greater trust that grows from a deeper relationship with Him. Do you simply trust that He is working all things for the good of those who love Him (Romans 8:28)? Do you simply trust that He will answer and strengthen those that wait upon Him (Psalm 38:15, Isaiah 40:31)? Do you simply trust that God is near to the brokenhearted (Psalm 34:18)? If you are like me and have trouble trusting these things at times, cry out to God, "I believe; help my unbelief!" As C.H. Spurgeon wrote, "Oh, that we had that uncommon faith to take God at His word!" Bring to Him every doubt in your heart, and by His Spirit He will work to produce in you that simple faith by His abundant grace, and for His own glory.

Dear Lord, You know the wickedness of our hearts. We are naturally inclined not to trust You. It is only by Your grace that we may trust You. I pray that, by Your mighty Spirit, You would produce in us a greater faith, to simply take You at Your word. We thank You and we praise You for the gift of saving faith we have through Jesus Christ, and for that holy communion that we get to have with You today and for all eternity. What a gracious God You are, O Lord, as we have tasted and seen.

I pray now for the reader, that he or she would turn to You in simple childlike faith, not doubting. Lord, You have said that Your power is perfected in weakness, and we are very weak. Show Your power through us, that we would experience Your wonderful grace and mercy and be filled with joy as we look to You as the fountain of living water, which makes our hearts glad. God, glorify Yourself through the reader in whatever suffering he or she might be experiencing, as others look and see that Christians do not grieve as those without hope.

We love You, God, and we want to know You more. As the deer pants for streams of water, so our hearts long for You, O God. Make us more zealous for Your glory, and help us to trust in Your sovereign plan. We pray these things for Your glory, in Christ's name. Amen.

BENJI'S JOURNEY

We asked the children if they wanted to write something in the book, and Hannah wrote this as her contribution. It is touching for us to see what she went through as a little girl trying to make sense of why her brother had died and also to see her childlike faith in the hope of heaven in Christ.

Below are her words, and on the following page are images of her handwritten thoughts.

My name is Hannah. I was born thirty-nine days after Benji died. At first I didn't understand about how Benji died. I thought he had been electrocuted, and when I was about one or two years older I thought he died of diabetes. Later I found out how he had actually died. In kindergarten, sometimes I would get upset at school looking at the metal picture of him in a little garden they made for the students who had died. But if you think about him in heaven looking up at God and giving Him a huge smile, it makes you feel better. God had a journey for Benji, and in that journey was death. But part of the journey is the end, even at a young age.

Hi. My name is Mar...
I was born ... days after
Benji died. At first I did...
understand about how Ben...
died. I thought he had
ben electricuted and
when I was about one
or two years older
I Thought he died of
diabetes. Later I fou...
out how he had actu...
died. In her der Garden some...
I would get upset at scool
looking

at the medler picture of
him in a little garden
they made for the students
who had died. But if you
think about him in heaven
looking up at god and giving
him a huge smile it makes
you feel better. God had a jerne
for Benji, and in that jerne...
was death. But part of the
jerney is the end.
even at a yang a age.

~ Benjamin Samuel Easler ~

CPSIA information can be obtained
at www.ICGtesting.com
Printed in the USA
BVHW010817081119
563185BV00003BA/34/P